Indigenous Quotient/Stalking Words
American Indian Heritage as Future

Juan Gómez-Quiñones

Aztlan Libre Press
San Antonio, Texas

First Edition

San Antonio, Texas
210.710.8537
www.aztlanlibrepress.com
editors@aztlanlibrepress.com

Dedicated to the promotion, publication and
free expression of Xican@ Literature and Art

Publishers/Editors:
Juan Tejeda
Anisa Onofre

Veteran@s Series

Gómez-Quiñones, Juan.
       Indigenous Quotient/Stalking Words: essays
       ISBN-10: 0-9844415-2-2
       ISBN-13: 978-0-9844415-2-5
       1. American Indian History 2. Chicano/Mexican History.
       3. Native American History. 4. Indigenous Philosophy
       5. Mexican-American History 6. American Indian
       Culture and Education

Library of Congress Control Number: 2011936184

Cover Artist Statement: "This drawing (*Memories*) was done in 1992 and is part of a triptych created to commemorate the quincentennial – the year when Columbus arrived and allegedly "discovered" America. With this drawing, my idea was to depict the strength of our indigenous women and what they have endured to survive. They have never forgotten and are constant reminders of the atrocities of that conquest. The crosses symbolize generations of those whom we remember."

Memories has the following quote by Eduardo Galeano written across the top: "My memory will retain what is worthwhile. My memory knows more about me than I do; it doesn't lose what deserves to be saved." In the cover art detail for this book, the artwork has been reversed.

Cover Artist: Malaquias Montoya was born in Albuquerque, New Mexico and raised in the San Joaquín Valley of California. He was brought up in a family of seven children by parents who could not read or write either Spanish or English. The three oldest children never went beyond a seventh grade education, as the entire family had to work as farm laborers for their survival.

Montoya graduated from the University of California, Berkeley in 1969. Since then, he has lectured and taught at numerous colleges and universities in the San Francisco Bay Area including Stanford and the University of California, Berkeley. He was a Professor at the California College of Arts and Crafts in Oakland, CA for twelve years; for five of those years he was Chair of the Ethnic Studies Department as well. During this period he also served as Director of the Taller de Artes Gráficas, in East Oakland, where he produced various prints and conducted many community art workshops. Since 1989 Montoya has held a professorship at the University of California, Davis, teaching both in the Department of Art and the Department of Chicana/o Studies.

Montoya's classes at Davis include silkscreening, poster making, and mural painting, with a focus on Chicano culture and history. His own works include acrylic paintings, murals, washes, and drawings, but he is primarily known for his silkscreen prints, which have been exhibited internationally as well as nationally. He is credited by historians as one of the founders of the social serigraphy movement in the San Francisco Bay Area in the mid-1960's. Montoya's unique visual expression is an art of protest, depicting the resistance and strength of humanity in the face of injustice, and the necessity to unite behind that struggle.

For more information about Malaquias Montoya, please visit his website: www.malaquiasmontoya.com

The Mexica/Aztec singing symbol on the title page and its adapted talking symbol version used in "Stalking Words" were taken from the Códice Borbónico. The hand symbol used in "Indigenous Quotient" is a flat stamp from San Andrés Tuxtla which was taken from the book *Design Motifs of Ancient Mexico* by Jorge Enciso. Thanks to Robert Poschmann for his help in adapting these symbols for use in this book.

Many thanks to Rebekah Ann Horse Chief (Southwest Regional Studies Center, University of New Mexico), and Beatrice Lewin Deming (Law, UCLA) for reading the manuscripts. I appreciate Semillas Sociedad Civil for their support, as well as the support of Dr. T. Durán, Director, and the staff of the Southwest Regional Studies Center, University of New Mexico.

The content of these essays is the responsibility of the author.

DEDICATION

For the spirit and blood of the students, teachers and staff of Academia Semillas del Pueblo, and in particular the leadership of maestros Marcos Aguilar and Minnie Ferguson, El Sereno, California.

Tlapializtli	Se preserva por acción
Yuhcatiliz	Ser así es vida
In ahuehuetl	Gran árboles
in pochtl	de autoridad
Tlilli	Negro y rojo
tlapalli	señala sabiduría

TABLE OF CONTENTS

INTRODUCTION

In the essay "Indigenous Quotient," Professor Gómez-Quiñones provides a critique of Western hegemonic historiography on
American Indigenous Peoples, which has historically been used
to rationalize colonization and neo-colonization. Subsequently, in
the essay "Stalking Words," Gómez-Quiñones argues for intellectual theorizing and pedagogy to be rooted in Indigenous ethos as
a means of producing research that provides readers an awareness
of Indigenous heritage, as well as past, and current, discrimination
and exploitation.

"Indigenous Quotient" depicts the history of academic discourse
on American Indigenous Peoples. Gómez-Quiñones chronologi-
cally examines the context and purpose of Western discourse, specifically U.S. and Spanish/Mexican, on Indigenous peoples, which
demonstrates a continued attempt by Western intellectuals to rationalize colonization from Columbus to current proponents of
financial globalization. Gómez-Quiñones concludes by calling for
a paradigmatic epistemological shift towards Indigenous peoples
that negates the construction by European colonizers, which has
continued to be perpetuated by their colonial and neo-colonial descendents.

"Stalking Words" begins where "Indigenous Quotient" left off by
developing a paradigm rooted in Indigenous ethos that consists
of: l) critiquing colonialism and all oppressive power structures; 2)
self-reflection of historiography, theory, and philosophy; 3) responsibility of transmitting heritage; 4) Indigenous epistemology as the
foundation of personhood and auto-validation; and 5) ideological
autonomy. By establishing these tracts as a foundation for intellectual theorizing, Gómez-Quiñones points students and researchers
towards theory that also serves as a pedagogy that teaches the values and ethics of compassion and understanding, or as he states it,
"of strong heart and wise character."

Consequently, in these two essays, Gómez-Quiñones argues for
readers to connect to the intellectual traditions of an ever-present

American Indigenous civilization. With this new consciousness of Indigeneity, readers can better understand the intellectual and cultural heritage of all peoples in the Western hemisphere as a continuation of millennia of history and civilization. As such, Gómez-Quiñones demonstrates that Indigenous history is U.S. and Western hemisphere history and vice-versa. A critical understanding of this is a necessary requirement for any useful understanding of the history of culture, politics, and economics in the Western hemisphere. Finally, Gómez-Quiñones' essays demonstrate the necessity of the fundamental Indigenous "belief in the interdependence of all life and life sources." This depicts the historic and present responsibility all humans have to each other and their environment. Academics and intellectuals share this responsibility and this value should guide their, and our, understanding of all human action broadly, and history specifically. Also, all humans share the responsibility of upholding the rights to democracy, heritage, and self-determination, and Gómez-Quiñones demonstrates that academics must also uphold these moral obligations, and Indigenous ethos and epistemology provide the intellectual means for this responsibility.

José Luís Serrano Nájera
UCLA History Department

PART ONE:

INDIGENOUS QUOTIENT

"They cannot represent themselves; they must be represented."
Karl Marx

"Nunca olvidaremos."
Fernando Alvarado Tezozomoc

INDIGENOUS QUOTIENT
IQ
COBRANDO CUENTAS FOR AZTLANAHUAC

 **Mapping**

American Indian[1] ancestries and heritages ought to be integral to K-12 curriculums and university explorations and graduate expositions for obvious reasons – contemporary universalist understandings.[2] I refer not to a special presentation, project option, or ethnographic appreciation here and there, but rather to the full integration of Native American histories and cultures into academic curriculums. The Indigenous voice matters, yesterday and today, in substantive pedagogical and philosophical discourses.

The matter is too often disparaged or challenged. Two broad arguments are raised against Native American historical appreciation and existential recognition: 1) Indian realities exist largely in the past and are thus best left to certified academics; and 2) Indian consciousness can be appropriated for any representational purpose by anyone.[3] Related to these are two other arguable convictions: a) that there is a lack of continuity between contemporary and historical Native American cultural practices; and b) that Native Americans are on a world scale insignificant civilizational presences. Ironically, these negative arguments are voiced at a time when Indian-related political actions receive unprecedented media coverage, and when Indian religion and spirituality has become a matter of intense interest in certain Indigenous, and other, circles.

I believe that observation and experience enable us to clearly appreciate the continuities that subsume a civilizational past and indeed a present. Today we are better informed to explore the range of Native American societies than at any time previously. Scholars now understand that Mesoamerican culture spans a broad range of cultural practices and beliefs, from the aesthetic to the zoological, from the past to the present. Our consciousness will be raised by a thorough education in Native American heritage, provided we address this subject with scholarly respect and without harm to anyone.

In this essay I challenge the historiography that promotes disparagement of Indian heritage and a fundamental denial of Indian's cultural contributions. These negative attitudes are propagated through, among other things, the use of a denigrating vocabulary. Words such as aborigenism in English and aborigenismo in Spanish are part and parcel of an anti-Indian ideological construction utilized by admirers of imperialism, as well as false liberal friends, who feign empathy while covertly supporting imperialist agendas.

To understand the origins of Aborigenism, let us understand time and space specifics: during the sixteenth century, Europeans invaded the Caribbean and Mesoamerica. These encounters are not fiction, they are historical facts. The encounters provoked an Indian perception and a European perception. Only partialities are known of the Indian perception, but two mega-facts glare: one is that the Europeans were a disaster for the Indigenous; the other fact is that the Indigenous continue to exist and to experience the effects of the disaster. The Indigenous are responsible for themselves, as are Europeans, and between the Indian realities and the European perceptions lie bedrocks for transcultural understandings as well as for continued misunderstandings. We must acknowledge our mutual responsibility, and we must act. Encounters do not erase responsibility, but proactive resolutions may: Autonomy and Indigeneity.

A critique of the construction of European-premised appropriations and annexations must initiate the Indian question.[4] The responsibility for European actions belongs to Europeans. Europeans committed crimes as individuals, as well as on behalf of their governments and churches. As they entered first the Caribbean and then Mesoamerica, government agents for the mini-domains of Castille/Navarre ultimately became agents for the Hapsburg mega-monarchy, the closest entity to an overarching European political center at the time. And thus the exemplary "History of Conquest" waged by the European chieftains – Christopher Columbus, Hernán Cortés and all the others – was waged on behalf of Christian Europe for profit. These chieftains and their subordinates were Europeans, Christians, monarchists, and also profiteers. Thus a particular amalgam of the ideological, cultural, political, and economic comprised their sense of self, as well as their avowed group membership.

Colonial-inspired Aborigenism implicitly denies that Native American pan-cultural regions comprise one of the relatively few areas in the world from which a distinct culture, seminal to human development, arose.[5] Having inhabited Native America long before any North Atlantic contacts, Indians share a culture and civilization of great antiquity. A recognizable, documented, continuous cultural history began several thousand years ago when the Native American groups flourishing in northern and central lands built their societies. Indian peoples from the areas known today as the Southwestern United States and greater Mexico interacted throughout this protean cultural arena. Their shared cultural elements and visible historical structures were crucial to later cultural development. Colonialist's denial of the deep historicity of these people is central to the colonialist rationalization of conquest and genocide: Indians were savage and violent, period. Europeans were a deliverance; while for Indians, of course, Europeans were death.

Individual and group memberships, as well as conscious and semi-conscious identity constructions, inform arguments on behalf of the Indigenous with ironic twists. For those of us who are as unmistakably of Indigenous descent as our own grandmothers, to consider the Indigenous is on the one hand a form of self-interrogation. On the other hand, we live alongside an "Other" whose consciousness undeniably intersects with ours: I am a Mexican-Indian in the United States. One consciousness thus challenges the other. To paraphrase the poet alurista, self and critic are at once a creation and negation. As we learn, we fashion ourselves, become multiple. Once simply the insider, we are now also the examiner and the critic, plumbing the consciousness anterior to both. The cross-examinations may entail the knowledge that being Indian amounts to a single existential position. This stance requires respect, modesty, and sincerity. One must take care not to usurp the autonomy of Native American teachers, as so many other writers and thinkers have done in the past. The interrogative participants in this essay's dialogue are thus: 1) ourselves, the interior we; and 2) ourselves, the critics who function within society. We are Indigenous descendants, seeking the Indigenous. While using modes and formulations of the outsider, we indeed speak for ourselves, authentically; we attempt to transcend the dialogues that occur between us (the insider) and them (the outsider). Like others before us, we are here to challenge the contestations to Indigeneity. This means positively affirming our history; shaping our autonomy for envisioning the future; and rejecting with vigor all appropriators and falsifiers.

Specifically, this essay traces the aspects of intellectual and social Indigenous heritage that should be addressed in contemporary university curriculums. This is an ambitious consideration and if fully considered would entail an even more ambitious project than presented here. In this essay, my focus is selective and related largely to perceptions. The scale of the matter stems from the historical and sociological depth and breadth of the subject, the "vastness" of Native American peoples. In fact, what is being addressed when we consider the Indian question is a historical civilization that continues to exist in the present with all the complexities of any other civilization, including those of gender and sexuality. The task is as urgent as the subject is vast. Yet the task is hindered by the pervasiveness of Aborigenism and the persistent falsifying of Indigenism – ideological patterns deeply rooted in the history of the European West.

 Confessions

One would think that educated people would learn to appreciate the Indigenous by immersing themselves in the sources through which the Indigenous wholly or partially represent themselves. Yet most writers discussing the European occupation of North America emphatically announce that there are few Native American sources, i.e., few witnesses. We need only consider certain sources to see that this is not the case; and we need to learn to distinguish among the different sources, European and Indigenous alike.

European sources are telling. For decades, aptly named "Conquista" writings have been a staple in "Spanish" departments in United States colleges. What these sixteenth century chronicles offer is a triumphalist history riddled with literary justifications. As fine historical examples of colonialist pathology, they now show up in comparative literature programs. Upon examination, what is clear are the politics these writings convey to undergraduate students slated to become teachers and administrators. All the pathology of Aborigenism is contained in the substantive or tentative assertions of the writings of a slaver, Columbus (*Diario*), who served his apprenticeship as "discoverer" and grand admiral by learning the seagoing slave trade.[6] As Columbus prays, the Indigenous merit, desire, and appreciate servitude. To be sure, Columbus' own writings reveal a grandiose and avaricious man, a less than competent sailor and commander, and an enthusiastic ideologue for Europe, monarchy, and popery. In his perspective, the aggressor/invader/colonizer acts for altruism, while the victim/defender/colonized acts criminally. There are politics to be learned here.

A particularly egregious example of the foundations of Aborigenism is the canonical status of Hernán Cortés' self-serving writings, *Carta de Relación*.[7] Indeed, Cortés left a literary heritage alongside his political and social legacies. Like other founding "lieutenant colonialists" who sought to maintain their office vis-à-vis temperamental supervisors, Cortés faced two challenges: 1) to affirm his own superiority while simultaneously affirming the superiority of his superiors; and 2) to affirm the willingness of Native Americans to be both emancipated and subjugated by the European invaders. As it happened, Native Americans steadfastly declined such an invitation and condition. Thus Cortés, an unabashed colonialist, dwelled repeatedly on invented Indigenous qualities, and in passing rationalized that Indians were worthy enemies and hence appropriate subjects. Invariably, colonialists assure you that the colonial is a worthy subject who is best dealt with as an object. Indeed, European ends demand that Indian actions validate European triumphalism.

From the start, Cortés boldly sought to establish Moctezuma's willingness to be a vassal, a compliant vassal that Cortés could deliver to his superiors. According to Cortés' representation, the best sign of this willingness was Moctezuma's alleged "donation" of Mexico as a "free gift" "given" to the Europeans. In order to comply with European definitions, Cortés designated this state as a "kingdom" or an "empire," with Moctezuma acting as a "king" who, like other "kings," could give his possessions away.

According to the needs of Renaissance statecraft, states mattered, nations and peoplehood did not. Thus Cortés could claim to triply subdue an empire: receive one and offer one, and along the way introduce a whole series of misrepresentations of Aztec governance to serve his, and later, colonialist propaganda.

These Cortés/European-biased characterizations of the meeting of Europe and Native America represent to this day the majority of printed literature on the subject of "the discovery" and "the encounter." To the chagrin of some, the skeptical English scholar J. H. Elliott has delighted in underscoring the implausibility of Moctezuma, an Aztec leader, willingly donating the Aztec confederation to the unknown ruler of a distant and unknown political entity – especially given Aztec history, civic structure, or group characteristics.[8] But even as sarcastic historians recognize that many "donations" in European history are fabrications, they must also recognize the political purpose and context of the fabrications – and hence their "realness." Cortés fabricated his place and legitimacy by appropriating the Quetzalcoatl history and alleging that this powerful Indigenous lesson sanctioned European violence.

There are more than certain literary circumstances to be appreciated in the "conquest" literature of Europeans. Cortés modestly claimed to be only a translator – for God and a whole continent of people. He wrote his reports to benefit himself by unabashedly courting the favor of Charles V, the Hapsburg ruler of Europe, emperor of a constellation of entities and king of particularly important ones. We note that today immigrant and/or bilingual Indian children are sometimes denigrated intellectually by the accusation that they have no language. Let us recall that the one person in sixteenth century history who spoke only his own language, nearly unintelligible to others, was Charles V. His agents made Indians and their children learn the language of dominance, but Indian languages as well as symbols persist, while Charles' are arcane.

The verbal information that Cortés received in his dealings with the Aztecs allegedly came through not one but two interpreters, a male European servant and a female Native American servant. In the process of translation, these servants added their own biases to the ample biases of Cortés; Cortés added further biases in re-translating; and Charles, or his advisors, further distorted the communication. Through the labyrinths of translation, then, Europeans invented an America to suit themselves and constructed an imaginary Indian compliance.

Cortés was clearly motivated by self-aggrandizement, whether grudgingly accepting the Aztecs as somewhat familiar Moors, or disparaging them as barbarians, i.e., non-Europeans. Cortés' point was that Europeans have or should enjoy tutelage over them if only because of state superiority. As Voltaire snickered, Charles' political realm was neither holy, Roman, nor an empire, but rather a mafiosi inheritance gained by hook and by crook, the imagined claim of one usurper, Charles. Yet "translated," this bag of goods was indeed a European political entity. In fact, for Charles, there was no "Spain," politically or legally, nor would there be for two more centuries; there would be no claim to the higher loyalties of the Hapsburg subjects and their later descendants, because neither he nor they shared them. In the sixteenth century, the loyalties of imperial henchmen ascended in order from lord to overlord to capo di tutti i capi. They were gangsters who rationalized and translated their gangsterism. A fine example is Cortés' personal secretary, F. López de Gomar, who invented his share of lies about the Indigenous – thereby proving a twentieth century propagandist saw that the bigger the lie, the more people will believe it.[9] Not only a henchman but also a blasphemer, F. López de Gomar fabricated the lie that Indians believed the invaders were gods, which explains, no doubt, why the invaders were killed (*Historia de la Conquista*). No Indian would mistake Cortés the ruthless for Quetzalcoatl the moralist. Thus we learn about the importance of lies in the construction of domination. We may also learn of the interpretive impoverishment effected by premeditated absences and lacunae. Except in the records of priests and later the Inquisition, there was no reporting on expressions of gender and sexuality other than leers. The scope of Indian gender and sexual relations was beyond the gangster's ken – what they understood was concubinage and rape.

During the European invasion of Mesoamerica there was no narrative produced by Europeans with so much as a claim to objectivity; there is none today. The "great encounters" representation fiction turned to myth. Inspired by simplistic fictions and Medieval and Renaissance storytelling, Cortés, like other authorities, knowingly wrote fiction. As a multi-part, multi-authored novel, Cortés' writings present Aztecs in the context of European melodrama. Yet Cortés' version and justifications, his genre and agenda, remain current in the history of the European encounter, and nearly all the textbooks used in university classes today continue to present Cortés' version. We understand today that Cortés' actions on behalf of Europe were nothing less than a military invasion, a continuation of the European cultural heritage of endemic warfare. Yet one of the European's preferred accusations against Indians was that these recalcitrant others, who refused to be liberated, were violent. Here the victims of violence are conjured as violent. Cortés, like Columbus before him, was inspired by the so-called Crusader's aggressions against Muslims and Muslim lands – aggressions which, according to the writings of European participants, included the slaughtering of natives and, lo and behold, the eating of human flesh.

 **Amoral Moralizing**

Throughout recorded time, charges of cannibalism have frequently appeared in writings on encounters between peoples.[10] Although some depictions are quite embellished and imaginative, factual reports do exist of white humans eating other humans, including instances during the invasion of the Americas, such as during the 1528 Pánfilo de Narvaez expedition (Álvaro Núñez Cabeza de Vaca, *Naufragio*).[11] Yet Europeans, whether crusaders or historians, have conveniently and repeatedly set aside their own documented past on the subject; instead, they have launched a steady barrage of allegations of cannibalism among Native Americans – despite the near absence of credible first person accounts of this behavior.

Images of cannibalism are embedded in human ritualistic constructions and sexualized longings, specifically evident in Judeo-

Christian legacies. The cultural, economic, and sexual are neatly bundled within the charge of cannibalism. Alleged practitioners are of course subhuman, which means of course that they, their kin, and their property are fair game for the civilized. Literally and figuratively, as colonialism spreads, Europeans devour the natives. Yet from the beginning, Europeans targeted Indians as cannibals; Indians were left to atone and compensate. The allegations of cannibalistic practice among Native Americans created a universally endorsed cultural stigma and served as evidence of a fundamental inferiority that prima facie underscores the superiority and rationality of Europeans.

The charge of cannibalism is often linked to ritual killings or to the sacrifice of humans in religious rites. It is worth noting that there are no credible historical European eyewitness accounts of ritual killings among Indians. The European sensitivity to this issue is understandable given their own extensive familiarity with ritual murder – whether from their Bible, their Roman heritage of mass spectacle killings, their attachment to public executions, their obsession with warfare, or their extensive practice of religious and ethnic persecution culminating in the torture and death of alleged apostates, nonbelievers, or minority others by the score, or by the millions. Such is the history of European descendants.

 Such Friends

During the construction of a colonial society in Mexico, a pejorative image of the Indigenous was cultivated by would-be benefactors as well as explicit detractors. Actually, I doubt there have been any real benefactors vis-à-vis Indian peoples – although many have claimed to be. Some of their names may be familiar to students of the colonial Americas. Two sixteenth century priests, Bartolomé de Las Casas (*Apologética, Historia de las Indias*) and Vasco de Quiroga (*Documentos*), figure prominently.[12] Given the Christian avowals of Europeans and their hypocritical leaders, one would think that others would have shared these two men's limited advocacy on behalf of Indians – i.e., their recommendations against abusing Indians to the point of their demise. European leaders are nearly always represented as pious, when in fact they thrived on violence, debauchery, and avarice. Christian ethical commitments, clearly stated in the Ten Commandments and the Sermon on the Mount, were supposed to be followed in the construction of colonies. They were not.

Instead, the practices of colonialists were consistent with the real "Christian" values of colonial society and governance: avarice and violence. Vasco de Quiroga – an effective organizer of Indian labor – has been touted as a reformer and visionary, while in fact he was neither. Las Casas, inappropriately heralded as a defender of Indians, was in practice a defender of church prerogatives over the Indians. His arguments favoring somewhat better treatment for certain Indians (provided that they did not rebel) were in contradistinction to those of other privileged individuals in the colonial system who believed that, peaceful or not, Indians should be treated like blacks, i.e., Africans – and thus exploited to the maximum and punished ruthlessly. Both arguments had their day and space.

Although usually presented in terms that placed them on the same side – that of the angels – Las Casas and Quiroga were actually argumentative opponents; they agreed that the Indians must serve a colonial purpose, but they differed on how. Matters pertinent to Indians not only preoccupied colonialist field operatives such as these two priests, but also major system-wide ideologues such as Juan Ginés de Sepúlveda, Francisco de Vitoria, and Francisco Suárez. These three men affirmed limited protection for Indios and argued for their usefulness as productive unremunerated labor for both church and state. Nonetheless, the ideologues considered Indians fundamentally barbarian. In the Indian business, the church did well for itself, as did the state. There is a lesson in pragmatism here.

 **Child Labor**

Vasco de Quiroga actually sided with Hernán Cortés and his descendants, firmly arguing in favor of the cliché that Indians had benefitted from the "conquista." Indians thus, in his view, owed a debt that should be repaid. He objected to certain kinds of sales but not to slavery, the sale of human beings, which he saw as natural and beneficial. Neither Quiroga nor Las Casas could be considered humanist or humanitarian in the traditional sense – i.e., empathetic, tolerant, and privileging personhood. Nevertheless, Christian missionizing in the Americas appeared this way to certain mid-twentieth century scholars, such as Silvio Zavala and Lewis Hanke, both of whom wrote amidst the particular pro-Christian biases of the Cold War.[13] Quiroga and Las Casas contributed to the ideological view of Indians as inherently childlike and submissive. As perpetual minors and dutiful laborers, Indians were considered worthy of church ministrations. The Indian was, in other words, sufficiently endowed for catechism but not for civil standing. According to the prescribed benign scholastic view, Indians are children, and according to the economic practical view, they are children whose labor is useful. Thus the Indian is a bonafide subject rather than a ward.

These quasi-theological juridic views and rationalized prejudices persist in scholarship and media to our day. Quiroga and Las Casas were in basic agreement with other colonialist ideologues, such as the professional churchmen Juan Ginés de Sepúlveda, Francisco de Vitoria and Francisco Suárez.[14] As they believed Indians did not possess civil society, i.e., organized legal arrangements for their own governance, they believed that Indians could not perceive rights. Initially, Indians existed in a legal limbo; later their non-political status was considered indefinite. Contradictions in colonialist views did not impede their implementation. Indians may not have seemed organized enough for their own governance, yet somehow they were sufficiently organized to "gift" Europeans donations and recognitions that committed them and generations of descendants. In any case, a display of juridic colonial innovation could recommend a civic "limbo," a suspension. Contradictions abound, we learn.

According to denial arguments, Indians have no politics. Instead of governance, Indians were said to have "authorities"; instead of laws, chieftains; instead of resistance, violence. Europeans often argued that Indian bellicosity remained unorganized and that most Indian groups lacked even tyranny as a form of governance. Hence, by their own failings, Indians could not be the beneficiaries of rights. This argument not only underlined Indian's alleged inferiority, but in addition, allowed Europeans to "order them." The case was even made that Indians needed protection from other Indians, and that this responsibility fell upon the Europeans. The church hierarchy and missionaries thus faced innumerable tasks, including tending to Indian welfare. In contradiction to their own history, Europeans believed themselves predisposed to an orderly society rooted in legal principles. In truth, the ideal colonial state functioned as a prison system, and its missions resembled well-managed, productive concentration camps.

In the European view, improvements could perfect the colonial state but not replace it; the ideal was a well-ordered "republic" with segregated civil status under church and crown.[15] Within the colonial universe, Indians merited the attention of Europeans through vigorous and competent work – work that was to everyone's benefit, certainly the benefit of church and state, and also, of course, Indians themselves. In short, the Indian was not an exotic; rather, the Indian was a worker.

 Differences Becoming

Today's Indigenous are culturally and biologically quite a mixed population, and the fact of mixture has drawn attention to Mexico since the sixteenth century. Many Mexicans take a strong interest in their Indo-Mestizo roots, while Mexican scholars investigate the implications of their hybrid past and phenotypical appearance. Hybridity inspires definition.

In colonial societies, hybridity was both a social fact and an ideological stance, a source of contradictory resolutions.[16] By the late seventeenth century, some culturally distinct individuals and social pockets of colonial society were characterized as neither pre-European nor European; hybrids predominated. The subject of hybridity provoked both recognition and denial. Since the native-born carried the memory of Mesoamerica as Indian past(s) and Indian land(s), and since Indians remained, this memory compelled a reckoning. Yet retaining the Indian memory amidst a colonial social formation was a challenge, given the many attempts to obfuscate or manipulate this memory. Various arguments vis-à-vis hybridity have been articulated since the colonial era. Manipulators turn mestizajeism into neo-colonialism. Indigenous culture and identity persist as irreducible social processes spanning generations. In retrospect, many historical observations have been no more than imagined prognostics. Indian memory is both transhistorical and definitively historical.

 Social Process

There is no doubt that Indians left sources, messages, and communications that continue to be examined and debated today. Insisting on an Indian presence, various Indian-related communicators and writers asserted themselves. Fernando Alvarado Tezozomoc, *Crónica Mexicana* (1590s), wrote a conscious message concerning the past for the sake of the future.[17] And foremost among those in transmitting the past for the sake of the future were the nearly anonymous Indigenous informants and commentators whose testimonies were subsumed in the informative works of Bernardino de Sahagún, *Historia de las cosas de Nueva España* (1570s).[18] There is no way of knowing to what degree their recordings and interpretations have been transmuted in the translations of Sahagún, but information and assertion are there. This is undoubtedly true even for the less dependable *Historia de las Indias de Nueva España* (1570s) by Diego Durán, which stresses the achievements of the European clergy while providing some ethnographic information.[19]

Indigenous messages also appear in non-literary forms, from stelae to enormous monuments, from visual designs to oral myths, from danza tracings to urban edifices. There also exists a relative abundance of colonial records of Indian representation in petitions and in civil and criminal matters. Artifices and contaminations aside, these documents serve as useful evidence of the colonial social process and are quite distinct from the self-conscious articulations of intellectuals, whether Mestizos or Criollos (native-born Europeans). It is thus possible – though seldom achieved – to construct a view of the Indian that amalgamates past and present.

The relative inattention to this subject is due not to an absence of sources, but to an insufficient understanding of these sources.

 **Only Politics**

Indigenous politics confronted the first Europeans, and Indigenous politics remained through the colonial decades. Colonial manipulation of Indians for political purposes harkens back to the tragedy of Cuauhtemoc, authored by Cortés, and to Cortés' quarrel with the Audiencia in 1526. There was also the buffoonery of his son, Martín Cortés, who, claiming Indian support, encouraged an operatic political conspiracy in 1568 to have himself made "king" of Mesoamerica. Such were the politics of the Europeans.[20] Among the first political operatives to appropriate the Indian past – as they had appropriated Indian lands and labor – were the Mesoamerican-born Criollo descendants of some of the sixteenth century European invaders. To protest their less favorable status vis-à-vis the colony's European-born, Criollo advocates upheld a mystification of alleged feudal values, patriarchalism and ultramontanism. These types also researched Indian accomplishments and through some weird mental alchemy claimed them as their own. Thus we arrive at the paradox of Indian historical glorification as the flip side of anti-Indian bias.

Rather than a fork representing two choices, Indigenous authenticity and constructed Aborigenism, the biases are intertwined – a figure eight rather than a single synthesis. From pathetically declining elite Criollo sectors in colonial Mexico came the cry that preference should be given to the "natives," and Criollos, of course, declared themselves native. A hundred years after Fernando Alvarado Tezozomoc, who had boldly harkened back to the past in order to dream of the future, Carlos de Sigüenza y Góngora (1645-1700) timidly rationalized the privileges offered to what he called "the criollo nation," i.e., his own group.[21] His historicized rationalizing resembled that of other middle-class intellectuals in colonial societies who feared becoming marginalized, when in fact they already were. Quite simply, Sigüenza's approach required a heroic history similar to those claimed for their European homelands, but also appropriate for Mesoamerica. So Sigüenza invented *Teatro de Virtudes Políticas* (1680s), a Europeanized version of Mexica/Aztec political history. This triumphal public commemoration recalled specific Aztec achievements, each foregrounded by a maxim representing what Sigüenza considered a political virtue. He concluded with a rhetorical flourish equating the Roman power wielder, Neptune, with the Mesoamerican ethical teacher, Quetzalcoatl. Sigüenza, of course, had no political vision beyond his service to colonial authorities and no Indian identification beyond his choice of subject. He remained thoroughly grounded in European mythologies and lost his enthusiasm for dead Indians after witnessing a riot by live ones in 1692, when colonial authorities and symbols were attacked to shouts of "¡Muerte al gachupín!" At this point, Sigüenza knew who he identified with. His friend and colleague, Juana Inés de la Cruz, did comparatively better in representing, in her unique way, contemporary Indians in theater pieces, but that is the proverbial other story.[22] As for Sigüenza, his work remained consistent with reformulated European stories of European superiority and the rest of the world's inferiority. The Enlightenment reaffirmed the idea of Europeans as uniquely rational, and Sigüenza did not want to be lumped together with those who, according to Enlightenment luminaries, lacked a history, or at least a usable past.

Four decades after Sigüenza, the Jesuit Francisco Javier Clavigero turned more than a few pages when he set out to write *The History of Mexico* (his avowed nation) "By a Mexican."[23] Clavigero obviously thought this last phrase necessary. In his *Historia Antigua de México* (1760 ca.), he took the tack of steering the Indian persona in a more modern direction. According to his convictions, the merits of Mesoamerican Indians rivaled those of any other peoples. As Clavigero explained, the difference between the Indians of his day and those of the ancient past was due to Europeans; Indians had been condemned by force to a "miserable servile life." In effect, Clavigero was responding to disparaging Enlightenment writers – secondary ones to be sure, such as Georges-Louis Buffon, Abbé Guillaume-Thomas Raynal, William Robertson, and Cornelius de Pauw – who belittled

American natives, flora and fauna alike. Clavigero contested what these eighteenth century European scientists and sixteenth century European scholastics asserted: that Indians were innately inferior. Clavigero believed Indians to possess innate abilities, which he argued should be channeled in the direction of European skills and learning in order to ameliorate their negative conditions. He may not have convinced many of his fellow Criollos, but he was certainly among the earliest Mexican writers to contest Enlightenment biases and to equate the "humanism" of the Enlightenment with racism. During the same period, Juan José de Eguiara y Eguren included Indian manuscripts in the *Biblioteca Mexicana* (1760s), an ambitious catalogue as well as a scholarly advertisement that Indian knowledge and humanism belonged in a yet-to-be-instituted Mexican academy.[24] Following these precedents, the past was to be used in the future.

In the becoming of Mexico, a debate arose as to what was Indigenous and what was national. Around the turn of the nineteenth century, Fray Servando Teresa de Mier had little respect for Spaniards from Spain, but remained a loyal, if eccentric, Catholic colonial subject.[25] He argued that Indians owed nothing to Europeans, not even for Christianization. According to his Europeanized imagination, St. Thomas the Apostle – in the guise of Quetzalcoatl – had visited Mesoamerica, thus Christianizing the inhabitants during apostolic times. This argument does not resonate today, but in its time the theory was a clever sauce for the gander. Servando Teresa de Mier, and others like him, heralded a Criollo-Mestizo independence of sorts. The Indian was the coin used to purchase the passage to pre-modernity demanded by the illusion of an independent Mexico.

By 1810, independistas Miguel Hidalgo y Costilla and José María Morelos y Pavón both desired and feared the Indian.[26] These two populist independence leaders harbored a compulsive desire to know Indian languages and a compulsive belief that Indians were at the core of whatever Mexicans and Mexico might become. Hidalgo and Morelos probably were not free of biases, but in directly addressing the issue of Indian participation they represented a significant shift toward the political recognition of Indians. The flip side of the independista coin was Indian participation – including that of organized leadership – on the Royalist side. Having glorified the colonial subjugation of America, the weakened Royalists needed Indian allies. For a moment, Indians managed to negotiate benefits from the colonial authorities in crisis, as well as from independistas who sought to overthrow them. Indian's political status was acknowledged in statements of the movement for independence and in the liberal republican constitutions of Mexico in 1824 and 1857. Within the Mexican state, all persons were de jure citizens – which if nothing else demonstrates that Mexican policy makers were early adepts of modernistic hypocrisy. In evaluating the possibilities of neo-colonialism versus colonialism, we can draw the lesson that the wheels of justice are slow and not fine.

 **Names Are**

Among Latin American peoples and countries, only Mexico and Mexicans can, by their very designation, testify to irreducible Indianness. Whatever their meanings and interpretations, both Mexico and Mexica refer to the Indigenous. Yet Mexico's idealized national goals and character have retained a European stamp. Numerous post-colonial writers and programs sought to mediate the Indian reality, often in striking ways. Yet the contradiction of Indian versus European continued; in fact, between the 1820s and 1920s it may have worsened. Mestizaje accelerated and was ostensibly privileged while the privileging of the European remained and was perhaps accentuated. Finally, during a mid-twentieth century debate among a few interpretive Mexican writers, some progressive clarifications took place. These writers include Luis Villoro (*Etapas del indigenismo . . .*), Edmundo O'Gorman (*Invención de América*), Leopoldo Zea (*El Pensamiento Latinoamericano*), and Pablo González Casanova ("Sociedad Plural").[27] Their accomplishments, uneven though they were, weakened the European construction of Aborigenism that had hegemonically pervaded Mexican intellectual circles. Each was considered a progressive, each was Europeanized in a particular theoretical language; while learning to appropriate the language, they also learned to curse as intellectuals.

The basic premises of progressive writings need to be addressed critically, especially since certain core notions remain rhetorical weapons of choice vis-à-vis Aborigenism. Contradictorily and insightfully, the four aforementioned writers demonstrated a preliminary view of Aborigenism, i.e., the Indian as a historical construct. They also contributed to a modern view of Indigenismo, i.e., the central republic state and its agencies acting on behalf of Indian's integration into the majority national society. E. O'Gorman seminally and proteanly deconstructed the notion of "América" as a European historical invention and political manipulation. L. Villero, in particular, historicized the major stages of Indigenismo in modern Mexican history, thus enabling a precursory critique of these. L. Zea addressed the subversive and pervasive presence of European influences in formal thinking and conceptualization. P. Gonzales Casanova attacked the continuing colonialization of Native Americans and hypothesized other, then-novel conceptualizations. These four writers fomented a critique of Mestizo-ideologized, pseudo-reformist Indigenismo, implicitly heralding the crystallization of a more thorough critique. More to the point, among Indians themselves, the extant Indigenous intellectual heritages not only remained, they continued vibrantly. In the mid-1990s, Chiapas Indians took the critique further by rising in armed rebellion and setting forth their own plan for society and governance.[28] In their facsimile, the federal government of Mexico responded with armed force as well as an offer of negotiations. Circumstances encouraged the national executive and congress to propose a set of reforms partially favoring Indigenous rights. The candy of argument is nice, but direct resistance achieves quicker results. We learn rights are not to be accepted as gifts.

 **Amendments**

Guillermo Bonfil Batalla, author of *México Profundo* (1987), is welcomed as a major critic in Mexican anthropology who argues that Mesoamerican civilization is an ongoing, evolving, and undeniable force in contemporary Mexican life.[29] For Bonfil, the surviving

Indian communities, along with the "de-Indianized" rural Mestizo communities and vast sectors of the poor urban population, constitute México profundo. These communities, which remain rooted in Mesoamerican civilization, continually amend our understanding of the modern. An historical agricultural complex provides the food supply, the collective environment is maintained, and personal health is linked to positive human conduct. In short, work is understood as a way of maintaining a harmonious relationship with fellow humans and the natural world. Interdependence is inculcated through community service, which is considered part of each individual's life obligation. Participants in this arrangement believe that universal time is circular – origin-expansion-decline-transformation – and that humans, from birth to death, fulfill their own cycle in relation to other cycles of the universe. Bonfil believes that historical continuities provide future options.

Since the "invasion," Bonfil argues, the peoples of México profundo have been dominated by an "imaginary Mexico" imposed by the historical legacies and contemporary influences of the West. This ersatz society is imaginary, Bonfil argues, because it cruelly denies the cultural reality lived daily by most Mexicans. According to Bonfil there exists within México profundo an enormous body of knowledge, along with successful patterns for living together and adapting to the natural world. To face the future successfully, Bonfil argues, Mexicans must build on the strengths of Mesoamerican civilization, "one of the few original civilizations that humanity has created throughout all its history." Bonfil has written a powerful book that calls for a return to the source of history in America. He declares that there ought to be a sunrise to overcome a sunset.

The fact is, however, that Bonfil understates the pervasiveness of modernity in Mexico and underestimates how complicated and time-consuming it would be to peel away the layers of Western civilization from their Mesoamerican foundation. Such a regeneration would require negotiation and consensus on a continental level; yet Bonfil has little to say about the fact that Mesoamericans, migrating peoples, are today as transborder and transnational as they once were transcontinental. In the twentieth century, the Indians of Mexico traveled north, whereas their ancestors had traveled south. Today the combined populations of Zapotecs and Mixtecs, once found primarily in southern Mexico, make them the third largest Native American group in the United States. Moreover, many Mexican families evolved within Native American communities, and have coexisted with Indians for generations. Bonfil estimates that forty percent of the Mexican population is of wholly Indian descent and that another fifty percent has some Indian ancestry. Today, Indigenous families form an important part of both urban and rural Mexican-American neighborhoods. Many Mexican cultural practices, in short, are deeply rooted Indian beliefs and practices; on the other hand, Mexicans have committed an ample share of wrongs vis-à-vis Native Americans. To enliven the former and mediate the latter, Native Americans must communicate and act across borders of countries and neighborhoods, which they are.

 Neighbors

Where and what are the pedagogies here?[30] North of Mexico, the views of Indians and their historical relations are no less complex or protean. The large countries that inhabit the North American continent both arose through violence, have colonialist roots, and share certain modern biases vis-à-vis Indigenous. Yet racism, colonialism, appropriation, and exploitation are too often deleted from the history pages of the United States curriculums. Beatific rationalism comes into play, such as the "frontier thesis" that explained expansion as the advance of democracy, development, and individualism – when in fact what you had was violence, robbery and plutocracy. In the forming of the United States, Native Americans are important in several ways historically and thus these instances offer several learning experiences. During the English colonial period, Native Americans interacted extensively with Europeans and sometimes engaged in armed resistance against the colonial expansion into Indian lands. There were also sexual encounters of various kinds, the majority forced, some consensual. To be sure, Native Americans mixed with whites in northern North America but not on the same scale as in other parts of the Americas. A pattern emerged, first in the Caribbean and then on the mainland, in which Indians were removed and replaced by Blacks; the explanation offered was "Indian treachery."

To detect biased tracings one need only examine the pseudo-tragedy of Pocahontas and the fake heroism of the Pilgrim settlement myths. These explicit rationalizations of conquest betray the anti-Indianism of English-speaking whites. Their intolerance, ingratitude, avarice, and cruelty dates back to the first contact between Indians and Europeans in northern North America. Colonial governor William Bradford, writing in his history of Plymouth Colony, envisions the extermination of the Indians – even while noting that without the generous Indian donation of food stuffs the English colonists would have died.[31] Cotton Mather, a prominent clergyman of the colony, jealous for the site of New Jerusalem, extolled the burning alive of Indian men, women, and children. During the Enlightenment, the descendants of the early English colonists continued to reconstruct and rationalize their racism in the service of their personal and political independence. The lessons they applied made the first last. How do you like them New England apples? Late 20th century polemicist David Horowitz argues that the decimation of Native Americans in the 17th and early 18th centuries "forged" the thirteen colonies and was essential to the founding of an "American" nation and state. The Declaration of Independence commemorates "merciless Indian Savages." Thus genocide has its compensations.

Later history mimicked early history; the first minority would be the last minority. In encounters with the original colonizers, Indians were disparaged, pilfered, dislodged, demonized, and finally killed. English-speaking ideologues from the Pilgrim clergy to Thomas Jefferson commented on Native Americans, but they did not grant their commentary society-wide importance or consider it relevant to the task of "nation" building.[32] They did not even rhetorically debate whether Native Americans could be integral to the becoming of the United States. Their "no" was without ideological discussion; from the start, their actual commitment was to building a strong state for whites – a government, not an integrated nation. Such an entity was simply not envisioned.

Rather than improving, Indian status arguably worsened after the English colonies gained independence. William Clark, who was commissioned by Thomas Jefferson and would later make expansionist history with Meriwether Lewis, wrote of an unremarkable encounter with a Native American party resulting in the killing of four men and four women and the seizing of two children, 16 horses, and 100 (pounds) worth of plunder. Jefferson's response: "We must leave it to yourself to decide [whether] the end proposed should be their extermination or their removal." Jefferson later wrote to another Clark, "Indian Fighter" George Rogers Clark, "The same world would scarcely do for them and us." Given the dire consequences the Lewis and Clark expedition augured, and the historical demise of Native sovereignty, the continued celebration of the expedition is a callous and cynical display of triumphalism.

One of the motives underlying the push for the independence of the thirteen colonies was a desire for Indian lands. Indeed, the acquisition, appropriation, and allocation of Indian lands would be foundational to capitalist development in North America. The dislocation of Indians proceeded apace. As the advance agents of white expansion traveled west of the Mississippi, their testimonies indicated that they labeled Spanish-speaking farming Mestizos Indians, and that autonomous Indians were more likely to face extermination than the former. After the 1830s, English-speaking elites took over the power, profits, functions, and celebratory symbolism of the Spanish-speaking elites living west of the great river. They also turned Indian peoples against each other. Not until the advent of the twentieth century did a legislative measure, the Snyder Act (also called the "Indian Citizenship Act of 1924"), specifically recognize Indian citizenship and Native American participation within local government. To be sure, Indians were to be isolated on reservations as well as in certain spaces of the public mind – and hopefully remain there.

Even as increasing numbers of people living in the United States claim an Indian identity for themselves, the majority remain badly ignorant of, or misinformed, about the history of the Native Americans on whose lands they walk. The 1960s did see the rise of Native American Studies and the dissemination of pioneering critiques of domination, but these developments failed to gain true momentum. Small university programs emerged, sometimes characterized by a few dominant academics, sans Indian pupils or Indian faculty.

All too often, the agendas for these programs were set by administrations rather than emanating from Native American communities themselves. Meanwhile, anti-Indian attitudes prevailed in the broader curriculum through the 1980s, despite claims of revisionism. For example, the classroom text by Tzvetan Todorov, *The Conquest of America* (1984), is popularly offered as revisionist.[33] Like the closet conservative Václav Havel, Todorov updates the rhetoric while delivering essentially the same message. Indian leaders are described largely as hapless foils for the masterful Europeans; Indian subjugation, though tragic, offers useful methodological keys for revisionist historians.

Disparagement of Indians also appears in the work of novelist Larry McMurtry. Here, the ten-thousand-year-old Indian is a sidebar to white nostalgia for the racist west of McMurtry's childhood. What could be more ironic than the colonialistic glorifier, Larry McMurtry, signing a pseudo-biography of Crazy Horse, the Indian commander? Actual realities are far more compelling. What can convey the story of the first Wounded Knee, South Dakota (1890), a massacre of Indians, better than the events at Pine Ridge, the second Wounded Knee, a siege of Indians nearly a hundred years later in 1973?[34] And is not the first Wounded Knee a representative history of all prior events in which Indians suffered violence at saber or rifle points? The decimation of Indian leadership is best exemplified in the daily biography of Leonard Peltier, an Indian leader whose fate was paraded before guards and their families – whites clamoring for ruthless punishment of the Indian, this militant Indian.

 **Peacemakers**

Evidence indicates that unlike Euro-Americans, Indians actually never preferred to draw simplistic lines between themselves and others. It was whites who taught Indians about group distinctions. While presenting themselves as blessed peacemakers, whites invariably sought to color Indians – ultimately settling on red, the color of blood. In their attempt to become more than a European color reference, Indians employed a variety of strategies – battles, fleeings, and even matings. Ultimately, the options for the future seemed to come strictly from the past: disappearance or servitude. Indians were placed in camps or removed and then placed in camps, accompanied by guards – dispensers of charity and thieves. Not just whites but other minority groups joined in the farewell, hoping the Indians would forever leave their lands behind. Indians have learned the price of "progress": a pound of their flesh.

Inspired by the advanced pragmatic philosophies of the English Enlightenment, Indians also received a lesson in laws and tithes. One explanation for the Indian's plight was their lack of a concept of property – they were simply not in sync with the English-speaking elite; which is to say that if Indians had private property, they, their goods, and their land would be respected today. Sure they would. Henry Knox (Secretary of War, 1788-1794) said that the Indians needed "a love for exclusive property" – then assigned to the War Department "all matters related to Indian affairs."[35] Another Secretary of War, John C. Calhoun – who was particularly attached to a particular form of property, slavery – added a Bureau of Indian Affairs (131A) to the War Department in March, 1824.

In 1849 the Indian Office was transferred to the Interior Department, which oversees land matters. This administrative shift signaled the beginning of large-scale efforts to relocate Indian groups to places away from their homelands, a harsh but telling action that characterized the next fifty years. The human rights and equities of Indians gave way to the "rights" and interests of others, from sea to shining sea. Given the general pattern of Indian accommodation to Euro-Americans in North America, these actions were as unnecessary as they were cruel. Not surprisingly, conflicts broke out across U.S. territories. In 1874, the largest armed encounter between Plains Indians and whites resulted in a resounding Sioux victory at Little Big Horn, Montana. In 1890, at Wounded Knee, South Dakota, U.S. army units avenged themselves in the massacre of weaponless Indian women and children – apparently none of them heirs of the Enlightenment. U.S. federalists were to avenge themselves again nearly a hundred years later at the same site. To understand the rise of the hegemonic United States, you begin with Indian histories and Indian lands.

 This Land

Here in the United States, there were no discussions on the souls of Indians or the possible wanderings of an apostle. By Acts of Congress in 1832 and 1866, the BIA claimed all matters pertinent to Indians; in fact, the Indians themselves belonged to the BIA.[36] Indians in the U.S. arguably had no constitutional rights, and Indian parents lacked even educational rights over their children. The Native American was emphatically not a United States citizen. The Dawes General Allotment Act passed by Congress in 1887 ended up reducing the land acreage allotted to Indians from 138 million acres to 48 million by 1932. The rationale was that by assigning Indian lands to individual family heads, Indians would become farmers and thereby strengthen themselves economically. However, unlike efforts to encourage farming in other parts of the world, Indian farming remained severely under-supported, under-irrigated and underfunded, judged by whites – a failed socio-economic experiment, a spurned "gift."

Indians did not fare much better in the twentieth century, despite token measures undertaken on their behalf. The Snyder Act of 1924 recognized certain Indians under certain conditions as U.S. citizens, and in 1934 the Howard-Wheeler Act ended the land policy of the Dawes Act and promoted the establishment of local tribal governments according to certain guidelines. By superceding more traditional forms of leadership, this latter development threatened the stability of whatever collective autonomous life remained among Indian groups. World War II ushered in a new age of rationalism for everyone, Indians included. According to the Termination Act of 1953, Federal Indian services and trusteeship, such as they were, were to be phased out, i.e., Indian land allocations were up for grabs.[37] The worst did not happen, i.e., complete displacement, perhaps because of publicity surrounding allegations of malfeasance and bribery of congressional staff connected to "Indian Affairs." Unfortunately, however, neither did congressionally appropriated money reach Indian families, at least for the most part. By the 1950s, Indians suffered over fifty percent unemployment and poor mortality, health, housing, and education rates and the indignity forced upon unforgiven enemies, the desecration of their dead and their ancestors.

In the 1968 Civil Rights legislation, the U.S. offered some non-specific recognition of Indian rights. Other congressional legislation almost made Indians the equal of whites by granting them conditional rights over the remains of Indian dead (although scientists can still claim Indian remains), and allowing some latitude for Indian religious practices. Despite the concessions, however, Indians suffered a loss of language and group identification; in short, they experienced "Americanization." The history of the Indians is a history of war – defeat, occupation, powerlessness, and dispersal. Native Alaskans and Hawaiians have experienced a similarly negative pattern.

At a press conference in the Soviet Union, Ronald Reagan, that ever-curious and philosophical student of history, wondered aloud whether the U.S. government had been too tolerant in its dealings with Native Americans.[38] His answer was that Indians would have been better served by forceful assimilation, in effect, cultural eradication. "Maybe we should not have humored [Indians] in wanting to stay in that kind of primitive lifestyle," Reagan said. Today there exist two dozen county-sized areas inhabited by Indians whose "lifestyle" is indeed deplorable – this courtesy of Reagan and his successors. In a misguided effort to correct this sorry state of affairs, some states have approved the development of Indian-run casinos, which seem to exist solely to assuage white boredom. Indians have been promoted from the circus tents to the gaming tables. However, since most people of Indian descent now live in cities, they are not likely to be the beneficiaries of casino dispensations.[39] They work for other dispensations or concessions. One hope for a true Native American paradigm and forum for Native American presentations is the inauguration of the National Museum of the American Indian.[40] Presentations should include exhibits on the Indian policies of each U.S. president.

 **Turning Around**

The point of learning about the Indigenous past is not to relive past practices, or to propose one essentialization over another, or to be immobilized by history. The first stone to demolish the old presidio is our own consciousness. Aborigenism, a colonialist construct that continues to be propagated in contemporary academic presentations, must be challenged. Of course, the colonialists and their colonialized lackeys prefer that this matter of Indian heritage and equities not be too pointedly discussed. Whoever brings up heritage linked to equity is attacked without the usual academic coyness. To respond to this bias will no doubt be considered an anti-bias; in anticipation of counter-charges, let me state that neither I nor any other reasonable person believe the "colonialists" to be universal, perennial, homogeneous conspirators. I believe they are simply colonialists. They follow their own interests in their own ways and in their own times. Today's colonialists express themselves in quite nuanced terms; as in yesteryear, not all are fully conscious of the ideological harm they do. They and their lackeys discuss colonialism and then slyly suggest that it cannot be defined. Even to critique colonialist degradations is not necessarily to be absolved of wrongs inherited or compromises made. The critique is not necessarily a defense of the critic. Although colonial projects may not have benefitted all colonialists directly, the fact remains that there was a usurpation of peoples from their land, along with a colonialistic rejection of this historical fact.

From Columbus to the present, Aborigenism has divorced native peoples from their land, culture, and ultimately themselves. Euro-American's writings on the "Other" are academic dominators seeking to recover intellectual ground momentarily lost to resistance writers; in academic and literary debates, pro-Native writings and writers are invariably dismissed as parochial or political. The academy is where schemes of domination are laid out; the Indigenous realm is the battlefield of struggle. To give credit to some anti-colonial critics, pioneering critiques of domination have appeared. Unfortunately, the early critics, whose personal circumstances often provided direct knowledge of the ways of domination, were typically superceded by those for whom domination was unfamiliar. The critiques thus became their own subject. In short, despite the occasional intertwining of the dominator and the dominated, the dominators have remained firmly in control of the academy.

One may conclude that people and land are joined or separated, more often than not, by political will; and to speak of one people or some peoples, is to imply another or others. Indian-European relations entail significant intellectual and social encounters from the first to the present. Human identities, whether Native American or European, are a construction. All attempts to define them remain as elusive as the subjects of the definitions themselves. Images of the Indian are no more or less than images; their seminal subjects are quite diverse and contradictory.

 A Spade

As the quincentennial anniversary of 1492 approached, the Indian question became politicized across the Americas and has become more or less universally acknowledged as a sensitive and partisan equation. It is not a matter of knowing the nuances of theory or the trends of superstructures. The individual Indian spades deep into the heart for that formidable strength that flows from the joining of belief and memory, from devotion to the future, for the sake of the past. The inalienable sovereignty of Indians transcends the niceties of civic recognition. Do they want to be caretakers of casinos and interrogants for ethnographers, or do they want to refashion their history into a call for autonomy and consciousness? Such questions vex academic authorities; the Indigenous, after all, are suspect from the deserts of Palestine to the jungles of Colombia. To take up the pen on behalf of Indigenous representation alarms those who see the shadows of swords on the walls, not of forts, but of academia. The wretched of the earth are not in liberal favor today. Yesterday and today, colonialists do not write for their subjects; their discourse is intended for their fellow colonialist club members. And colonialists become colonialists in part through intellectual bias. This includes even those of a liberal, seemingly empathetic bent who feign to offer critiques of past power relations while in fact rationalizing current ones.

Liberal academics are gatekeepers and proprietors; conservative academics are vigilantes. A keen political motivation lurks beneath their guardianship: the Indigenous are portrayed as "natives" as a means of reducing their full human citizenship or as a cue to an implied demonization. Fear and hostility are prime colors in this portrait. Both the sciences and the arts are complicit; references to works by "natives" in public policy discussions only bolsters state power over the Indigenous. Colonialistic academics do not engage in critical reflection of their affiliations; rather, they scheme over the graves of dead Indians and exclude live ones, especially those reluctant to "play" Indian. This pattern is quite evident in the academic coverage of colonial America through twentieth-century Wounded Knee. Colonialist writings are not entirely worthless; certainly they provide insight into colonialism's pathologies. However, these materials consistently betray a sense of cultural and ideological superiority over peoples of color from the Americas, Africa, the Middle East, and Asia.

A recurrent ploy in the academy is the manipulation of "differences": now you see them, now you don't. Historicity is exaggeration, but globalization is practical; human rights are imaginary but monetary profits are real. Among academics this approach allows for a fair amount of self-righteous posturing and finger wagging. Today's colonizers do not concede their sense of moral and intellectual superiority. Moreover, these intellectual descendants of the fashioners of apartheid and segregation actually decry distinctions between cultural spheres and civilizational zones. Now that cold war bipolarism has faded and supposedly a new single world order is afoot, racial and cultural differences are asserted passé. Never mind that serious students of human history have argued for some time that all cultures emerge and evolve in a process of hybridity and synthesis, cultural racial hierarchies continue.

Naturally, globalism allows for sub-market differences. Today's trade emanates from "the West," which generates the fictions of the East and South. Globalization has clear economic and political anchorings: financial capital, human labor and armed force. The sword and the dollar have created a global palimpsest of consumer-targeted and ideologically digested artifacts. For the Indigenous these are updated replays. The mandate, however, is being questioned. Some subalterns are rejecting hegemonic notions, old or new, and the rejection is becoming a worldwide trend, a future asserted.

In centering on Native American people and the Americas as a major site of human development and critical reflection, Indigenism insists on a primal subjectivity in opposition to Eurocentric objectification. If Native American Studies, or Chicana/o and Mexicana/o Studies fail to privilege philosophical, cosmological and ethnical Indigenism, it will be nothing more than an aggregation of courses that are micro sub-expositions of standard academic Eurocentrisms. Indigenism's basic existential premise is agency – validated by Indigenous concepts of governance, pedagogy, society, culture, and civilization – and its approach is fundamentally macro. It identifies a social context for knowledge, seeks information from direct sources, and continually links historical and contemporary realities. In so doing, Indigenism opens dialogues and constructs discourses that previously did not exist. It raises questions that lead to richer interpretations in three fields: 1) cultural/aesthetic; 2) social/behavioral; and 3) philosophical/cosmological. Although Indigenism is a positive stance privileging the humanity of all and a step toward intellectual and psychological liberation, it nevertheless arouses fears and apprehensions. The best response to this anxiety is the assurance that Indigenism is not a passing fad.

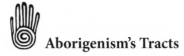 **Aborigenism's Tracts**

A fair desert wind must expose the tracts of Aborigenism in university discourse. Colonialism as an academic order continues to be expressed intellectually and conceptually as white academics conspire not to erase, but to represent the Indian graves scattered in the fair groves of academia. According to this order, dissidents or protestors are devils, while authoritarians of the order – whoever is the reigning Caligula – are saviors. As existence precedes essence, colonialization precedes Aborigenism, or rather reconfigures itself while remaining consistent in its hegemonic goals. In this world order, the colonialists audaciously seek to establish a post-twentieth century colonial mandate: tangible resources serve as objective motivators, while electoral protestations, often weak, serve as subjective motivators. In short, there is no post-colonial. The colonialists remain, spreading infectious disease like lepers without bells joining in the incantations of Allen Ginsberg's "Moloch"; but in contradiction to his invocations, theirs are in praise.

With its anything-goes methodological eclecticism, post-modernism only serves to rationalize this perpetual colonialism. Post-modernists tend to abhor attention to the historical Indigenous and to utopian change – one being too particular, the other too abstract. Ostensibly anti-political, post-modernism is in fact anti-humanist, anti-ethical and, ultimately, very political. Hermaphrodites, Hermeneutics, and Higher Returns have joined. A particularly cute aspect of post-modernism thinking is the denial of even itself and its own features. For example, it offers an ostensible critique of Eurocentrism and patriarchy while remaining adamantly Eurocentric and male dominated – its major theorists, Michel Foucault, Jean-Francois Lyotard, Jacques Derrida, Gilles Deleuze, are all European males. Post-colonialism is ersatz colonialism.

The lessons of repudiation need to be applied to false friends – not just post-modernism, which is centered mostly in apolitical European literature and art departments, but also to revisionist post-colonial and subaltern studies, which are ostensibly premised on activist-driven historical interpretations and political advocacy. While these revisionist pursuits do call for reconsideration and innovation, the point of departure remains the colonial.

To correct this problem, the pro-Indigenous say, you start prior to where the colonial began. You begin with what the colonial could not subdue or eradicate; you begin when there was some measure of cultural autonomy rather than subalternity. Geography must be foregrounded because real struggles occurred and occur in real spaces; that said, the effort is not to reclaim turf, but civic freedom and intellectual sovereignty. Personal hostilities are not mandated, but political and philosophical struggle for a free world is, for the sake of human survival, threatened by the past denial of equality, liberty and solidarity. If the Indigenous are expected to be spear carriers, are they not also the torch carriers – albeit not fully recognized as such? And should not the recognition be more widespread and emphatic that colonialism is not only indeed dying, but will be buried.

To reclaim the historical "irenunciable libertad" is to continue the unmasking of Aborigenism for what it is. This is not a literary exercise for literary audiences, it is a vital task of learning for the sake of human survival. The anti-Aborigenism effort should be discussed in neighborhoods as well as on campuses. Indian historical experiences, after all, teach about the construction of domination and how the loss of freedom comes about. From what is Indian, we learn of the beauties and pitfalls of being human; through studying the Indigenous, we show reverence for the past and advocacy for the future. Freedom for Indians is a prelude to the liberation of the Americas.

Transcendent over the events and details of Native American history in North America are the facts of Indian historical association with land as the home tenaciously claimed, the premise of the cherished culture, and as the deep love of Indian hearts, the inspirational incentive of Indian creativity.

The major modern states of North America are camped on Native American lands, in many cases their historically very recent jurisdictions intersect the habitats and territories of specific, single, historically rooted Native American groups. The claims of these modern states are premised on spurious concocted arguments of one variety or another. Ultimately justified on the basis of Euro-Judeo-Christian supremacisms, these claims are buttressed by pervasive racializations, whether neo-theological, proto-military, or pseudo-legal. Indeed, depriving peoples of their land on the basis of Christianization, discovery, economics, and militarism are potent concoctions. Certainly, herein at the juncture of historical presence and consuming avarice are core overarching pedagogies to be learned. All lessons have a premise.

The obvious initial unlawful and bellicose occupation of North American Indian lands by European invaders may explain why colonialistic apologists for the "New" world do not spend much academic energy in delineating the theft and suppression of Indian sovereignty in their self acclaimed "objective" scholarships. The gross magnitude of this crime serves as a perverse manipulation for its denial. The scholarly Juan Ginés de Sepúlveda is of course the alter voice for the soldierly, Bernardo Díaz del Castillo. Neither is distant from the twentieth century empire rationalizing economist, Walter Rostow, and he is in turn, if updated, the antecedent to the twenty-first century post-colonialist academic.

Modern liberals have constructed various Native American nations, not as warfare prone pagans, but simply as ethnic minorities. Hence, history as well as sovereignty are denied in the present century. Thus, Native Americans and Native American groups are only transitory "problems," solvable with a little more money and a slightly better administration from and by the dominating overstate. All three major modern states of North America and their antecedent colonial predecessors in fact have long histories of dealing with Native American societies as sovereign, or near sovereign, nations as evidenced by the numerous and recurrent negotiated compacts or treaties to which these Euro states have agreed, or the ongoing discussions they program with Native American representatives. The United States during the 19th century alone "ratified" over 400 treaties.

More valuable to Native Americans than these signatory episodes is the persistence of Indigeneity throughout North America. Indigeneity is, of course, associated with land consciousness and land loss and also more than even these, the sheer historicity of Native American cosmology and philosophy. For Native Americans, history, identity and ethics come together whether one looks at 1973 Wounded Knee (South Dakota), or at 1993 San Cristobal (Chiapas), and at many places in South America between 2000 and 2010 – all civic demonstrations against that domination that also has its history. But surely Indigeneity is also a response to the genocide that is at the core of colonialism. Today's resistance is the negation of yesterday's colonialism, persisting to today. Simply stated, existentially, the First Peoples persist. The modality is changing, let's quicken the rhythm.

Endnotes

1. In the two essays included in this book, the terms American Indian, Native American, Indigenous, Native, Amerindian and Indian are used interchangeably to refer to the Red People who were the original inhabitants of the Americas. These two essays focus primarily on the American Indians of North America.

2. University knowledge on Native Americans often seems primarily intended for the specialized. In any case, see H. F. Cline, ed., *Handbook of North American Indians* (1972-1975), particularly *Guide to Ethnohistorical Studies*, Vol. 12-15; also *The Cambridge History of the Native Peoples of the Americas*, Vol. 1 and Vol. 2 (Cambridge University Press, 1996-2000); and R. David Edmunds, et al., *The People: A History of Native America* (Houghton Mifflin, 2006). For a defense of how U.S. historians have explained Anglo-Indian relations, see Kerwin Klein, *Frontiers of Historical Imagination: Narrating the European Conquest of Native America, 1890-1990* (Berkeley: University of California Press, 1997); and Devon Mihesuah, ed., *Natives and Academics: Researching and Writing about American Indians* (Lincoln: University of Nebraska Press, 1998). On Native American societies before European contact, a start is Alice Beck Kehoe, *America Before the European Invasions* (New York: Longmen, 2002); for the aftermath of contact, see John E. Kicza, *Resilient Cultures: America's Native Peoples Confront European Colonization* (Prentice Hall, 2003). The United Nations staff has provided a widely used definition, one submitted by José Martínez-Cobo, the Special Rapporteur to the Subcommission on Prevention of Discrimination and Protection of Minorities. In the U.N. report, entitled *Study of the Problem of Discrimination Against Indigenous Populations*, Cobo states: "Indigenous communities, peoples and nations are those which having a historical continuity with pre-invasion and pre-colonial societies that developed on their territories, consider themselves distinct from other sectors of societies now prevailing in those territories, or parts of them. They form at present non-dominant sectors of society and are determined to preserve, develop, and transmit to future generations their ancestral territories, and their ethnic identity, as the basis of their continued existence as peoples, in accordance with their own cultural patterns, social institutions and legal systems." The definition of the International Labor Organization's Convention 169, Geneva, 1989 is also widely referred. Article 1 states: "a) tribal peoples in independent countries whose social, cultural and economic conditions distinguish them from other sections of the national community, and whose status is regulated wholly or partially by their own customs or traditions or by special laws or regulations; b) peoples in independent countries who are regarded as indigenous on account of their descent from the populations which inhabited the country, or a geographical region to which the country belongs, at the time of conquest or colonization or the establishment of present state boundaries and who, irrespective of their legal status, retain some or all of their own social, economic, cultural and political institutions."

3. This is a refrain found among some specialists on the western United States who point to significant economic changes from pre-European contact to the present. The same individuals might not question claiming a continuity of "English" history from pre-Roman times to the present. For a discussion on views of identity, see Hazel W. Hertzberg, *The Search for an American Indian Identity* (Syracuse University Press, 1971); and Michael Green, *Issues in Native American Cultural Identity* (P. Lange, 1995). For critique of questionable representation, there are: Philip J. Deloria, *Playing Indian* (Yale University Press, 1998); and Shari M. Huhndorf, *Going Native* (Cornell University Press, 2001).

4. That is to say that discussing European expansion begs the question of examining Native Americans. In fact, until recently scholars have discussed European expansion and colonialism without extensively discussing Native American societies, for example, Nicholas Canny and Kenneth Pagden, eds., *Colonial Identity in the Atlantic World 1500-1800* (Princeton: Princeton University Press, 1987); and Warwick Bray, ed., *The Meeting of Two Worlds, Europe and the Americas, 1492-1650* (Oxford: Oxford University Press, 1993). For a review of recent literature, see Susan Kellogg, "Encountering People, Creating Texts, Cultural Studies of the Encounter and Beyond," *Latin American Research Review*, Vol. 38 (2003). An insistent counter voice to the omission has been Neal Salisbury, "The Indian's Old World: Native Americans and the Coming of Europeans," *The William and Mary Quarterly*, Vol. 53 (1996). Also see Anthony Pagden, *The Fall of Natural Man: The American Indian and the Origins of Comparative Ethnology* (Cambridge University Press, 1982).

5. See Paul Kirchoff, "Mesoamérica: Sus límites geográficos, composición étnica y carácteres culturales," *Acta Americana*, Vol. 1, (1943); and for later extension of the conceptualization, see Basil C. Hedrick, et al., eds., *The Mesoamerican Southwest: Readings in Archaeology, Ethnohistory and Ethnology* (Illinois University Press, Carbondale, IL: 1974). A recent English language publication which narratively bridges pre and post colonial processes in the Americas is Jayme A. Sokolow, *The Great Encounter: Native Peoples and European Settlers in the Americas, 1492-1800* (New York: M. E. Sharpe, Inc., 2003); see also Alice Beck Kehoe, *America Before the European Invasions*. As to how non-Indigenous interpret Indigenous conceptualizations, see Gary H. Gossen, ed., *Symbol and Meaning Beyond the Closed Community: Essays in Mesoamerican Ideas* (State University of New York, IMS, 1986).

6. Christopher Columbus, *Select Documents Illustrating the Four Voyages of Columbus* (2 vols., London: The Hakluyt Society, 1930). For context, see John H. Parry, *The Age of Reconnaissance* (Cleveland: World, 1963); and Jared Diamond, *Guns, Germs and Steel: The Fates of Human Societies* (New York: W. W. Norton, 1997).

7. Hernán Cortés, *Cartas y Documentos* (México D.F.: Porrúa, 1963). See also the updated Spanish version of his letters, *Hernán Cortés Cartas...* (Madrid: 1993); and in English, *Letters from Mexico* (New Haven: Yale University Press, 1980). See also José Valero Silva, *El legalismo de Hernán Cortés como instrumento de su conquista* (México D.F.: 1965). As has been noted beginning with Bernal Díaz del Castillo, (Farrar, Straus and Giroux, 1956 edition) consistent with his character, Cortés lauded his superiors, not his subordinates. For one, see Rosa María Zúñiga, *Malinche: Esa ausente siempre presente* (México D.F.: INAH=CONACULTA, 2004).

8. J. H. Elliott, *Imperial Spain 1469-1716* (New York: Mentor Book,

1966), passim. And John Lynch, *Spain Under the Hapsburgs (1576-1700)* (2 vols., Oxford University Press, New York: 1964, 1969). For social history approaches to the European occupation, see Benjamin Keen, "Recent Writings on the Spanish Conquest," *Latin American Research Review*, Vol. 20 (1985).

9. Francisco López de Gómara, *Historia de la conquista de México* (México D.F.: Robredo, 1943), passim. This is part of a series of works by this author. See Ramón Iglesia, *Cronistas e historiadores de la conquista de México* [with prologue and introduction by Juan Medina], (México D.F.: Sep Setentas, 1972, 1st edition, 1942). The English version is edited and translated by Lesley B. Simpson, *Cortés: The Life of the Conqueror by His Secretary* (Berkeley: University of California Press, 1964).

10. On cannibalism, see W. Arens, *The Man-Eating Myth: Anthropology and Anthropophagy* (London: Oxford University Press, 1979); F. Lestringant, "Calvinistes et cannibales," *Bulletin de la Societe du protestantisme francais*, Nos. 1 & 2 (1980); H. V. Vallois, "The Social Life of Early Man: The Evidence of Skeletons," in *Social Life of Early Man* (Chicago: 1961); and for its early commentary, see Peter Hulme, "Columbus and the Cannibals," in *Colonial Encounters*. For recent discourses on that discussion, see Paula Brown and Donald F. Tuzin, eds., *The Ethnography of Cannibalism* (Washington, D.C.: Society for Psychological Anthropology, 1983); Peter Hulme, *Colonial Encounters* (London and New York: Methuen, 1986); and Philip P. Boucher, *Cannibal Encounters* (Baltimore: The Johns Hopkins University Press, 1992).

11. Álvaro Núñez Cabeza de Vaca, *Naufragios y Comentarios* (Madrid: Taurus, 1969). See also Donald E. Chipman, "In Search of Cabeza de Vaca's Route Across Texas: An Historiographical Survey," *Southwest Historical Quarterly*, Vol. 91 (1987); and Fanny Bandelier, *The Journey of Alvar Núñez Cabeza de Vaca* (Rio Grande Press, 1964).

12. Bartolomé de las Casas, *Apologética Historia Summaria* (2 vols., México D.F.: UNAM, 1967); *Historia de las Indias* (3 vols., México

D.F.: Fondo de Cultura Económica, 1951); *In Defense of the Indians* (Stafford Poole, trans. De Kalb, IL: Northern Illinois University Press, 1974); and Vasco de Quiroga, *Documentos* (México D.F.: Polis, 1939). See Silvio Zavala, *La utopía de Tomás Moro en la Nueva España* (México D.F.: 1957); and Marcel Bataillon, *Vasco de Quiroga et Bartolomé de las Casas* (Paris: 1965).

13. Silvio Zavala, *La filosofía política en la conquista de México* (México D.F.: Editorial Cultura, 1947); Lewis Hanke, *The Spanish Struggle for Justice in the Conquest of America* (Boston: Little, Brown & Company, 1965); and *Aristotle and the American Indians* (London: 1959). See also José Ma. Ots Capdequí, *El estado Español en las Indias* (Buenos Aires: 1952).

14. Juan Ginés de Sepúlveda, *Democrates, segundo, o de las justas causas de la guerra contra los Indios* (Madrid: Instituto de Vitoria, 1951); [See also *Tratados Políticos*]; Francisco de Vitoria, *Reflecciones sobre los Indios* (Buenos Aires: Espasa Calpe, 1946); and *Obras de . . .* (Madrid: 1960); and Francisco Suárez, *Conselhos e Pareceres* (2 vols., Coimbra, 1953). For the first, see Angel Losada, *Juan Ginés de Sepúlveda a través de su "Epistolario" y nuevos documentos* (Madrid: 1959); for the second, see V. Beltrán de Heredia, *Los manuscritos del maestro Fray Francisco de Vitoria* (Madrid: 1928). Suárez is often cited and was perhaps a more competent ideologue than the other two, but there exists no adequate secondary treatment in English other than in the *Catholic Encyclopedia*.

15. Many of the "documents" on the colonial governance of the Americas are idealizations. At one time historians relied on them for their narratives of colonial Latin American history. See C. H. Haring, *The Spanish Empire in America* (New York: Harcourt, Brace & World, 1963); Lewis Hanke, *Aristotle and the American Indians* (Chicago: Henry Regency Company, 1959); and J. H. Parry, *The Spanish Theory of Empire in the Sixteenth Century* (Cambridge: Cambridge University Press, 1940).

16. See Magnus Morner, *Race Mixture in the History of Latin America* (Boston: Little, Brown & Company, 1967); and Elizabeth

Kuznesof, "The History of the Family in Latin America: A Critique of Recent Work," *Latin American Research Review*, Vol. 29 (1989); or the older C. E. Marshall, "The Birth of the Mestizo in New Spain," *Hispanic American Historical Review*, Vol. 43 (1963). For changes among Indigenous, see Pedro Carrasco, "La transformación de la cultura indígena durante la colonia," *Historia Mexicana*, Vol. 25, (1975).

17. Fernando Alvarado Tezozomoc, *Crónica Mexicana* (México D.F.: Vigil Leyenda, 1944); see also Fernando de Alva Ixtlilxochitl, *Obras Históricas* (2 vols. México D.F.: 1965, 1st printing 1891). Consult on early colonial native born historians, Gloria Grajales, *Nacionalismo incipiente en los historiadores coloniales* (México D.F.: UNAM, 1961); Manuel Carrera Stampa, "Historiadores indígenas y mestizos novohispanos, siglos XVI-XVII," *Revista Española*, Vol. 6 (1971); and Georges Baudot, *Utopía e historia en México: Los primeros cronistas de la civilización Mexicana 1520-1569* (Espasa – Calpa, 1983).

18. Bernardino de Sahagún, *Historia de las cosas de Nueva España* (4 vols. México D.F.: Porrúa, 1956); and see Arthur J. O. Anderson, "Sahagún's Doctrinal Encyclopedia," *Estudios de Cultura Náhuatl* (Vol. 13, 1983). For commentary on colonial writings, see Charles Gibson, "Writings of Colonial Mexico," *Hispanic American Historical Review*, Vol. 55 (1975). In particular, see J. Jorge Klor de Alva, et al., *The Life and Work of Bernardino de Sahagún* (State University of New York, IMS, 1988).

19. Diego Durán, *Historia de las Indias de Nueva España e islas de la tierra firme* (2 vols. México D.F.: Porrúa, 1967). Classic histories of the "conversion" of the Indians are Robert Ricard, *The Spiritual Conquest of Mexico* (Berkeley: University of California, 1966, originally published in French, 1933); and John L. Phelan, *The Millennial Kingdom of the Franciscans in the New World* (Berkeley: University of California Press, 1956).

20. For the Martín Cortés conspiracy, see Luís González Obregón, *Rebeliones indígenas y precursores de la independencia Mexicana en* *los siglos XVI, XVII y XVIII* (México D.F.: Ediciones Fuente Cultural, 1952), pp. 126-200; the standard trial record is in Manuel Orozco y Berra, *Noticia histórica de la conjuración del Marquez del Valle: Años 1565-1568* (México D.F.: 1853).

21. For Carlos de Sigüenza y Góngora, see his noted work, "Teatro de virtudes que constituyen a un príncipe," which is in *Obras*, (Francisco Pérez Salazar, ed., México D.F.: 1928). For Sor Juana and Sigüenza, see Franciso López Cámara, "La conciencia criolla en Sor Juana y Sigüenza," *Historia Mexicana*, Vol. 6 (1957); and for both and others, see Irving Leonard, *Baroque Times in Old Mexico* (Ann Arbor: University of Michigan Press, 1971).

22. On Juana Inés de la Cruz' ethnic references, see María R. González "El embrión nacionalista visto a través de la obra de Sor Juana . . ." in Adelaida del Castillo, ed., *Between Borders* (Encino: Floricanto, 1990). An accessible work on this major intellectual figure is Octavio Paz, *Sor Juana Inés de la Cruz, Las trampas de la fé* (México D.F.: Fondo de Cultura Económica, 1983).

23. Francisco Javier Clavigero, *Historia Antigua de México* (R. P. Mariano Cuevas, ed., México D.F.: Porrúa, 1964). On Clavigero, see Anthony Pagden, *An Eighteenth Century Historian of Mexico: Francisco Javier Clavigero* and *Storia antica del Messico* (Leiden: 1983).

24. For Juan José de Eguiara y Eguren, see his work *Prólogo de la Biblioteca Mexicana* (tr. Agustín Millares Carlo, México D.F.: 1944). He is also an early writer on Sor Juana Inés. For the antecedent contextual cultural ambience of Juan José de Eguiara y Eguren, see Irving Leonard, *Baroque Times in Old Mexico* (1971).

25. His noted work is [José Guerra] *Historia de la revolución de Nueva España* (México D.F.: Imprenta de la Cámara de Diputados, 1922). There is also *Escritos Inéditos* (México D.F.: 1944). For commentary on Servando Teresa de Mier, see Jesús Silva Herzog, "Fray Servando Teresa de Mier," *Cuadernos Americanos* (No. 154, 1967).

26. For some English language references to the Indigenous aspects of the Mexican movement for independence, see Hugh M. Hamill, *The Hidalgo Revolt: Prelude to Mexican Independence* (Gainesville: University of Florida Press, 1966); and Brian Hamnett, "Mexico's Royalist Coalition: The Response to Revolution, 1808-1821," *Journal of Latin American Studies*, Vol. 12 (1981). Both authors have published additional material. For events, see the classic Carlos María de Bustamante, *Cuadro histórico de la revolución de la América Mexicana* (6 vols., 1823-1832); and also Jaime E. Rodríguez O, ed., *The Independence of Mexico and Creation of the New Nation* (Los Angeles: UCLA-LAC, 1989).

27. Luís Villoro, *Los Grandes momentos del indigenismo en México...* (México D.F.: El Colegio de México, 1950); Edmundo O'Gorman, *La Invención de América* (México D.F.: Fondo de Cultura Económica, 1958); Leopoldo Zea, *El Pensamiento Latinoamericano* (2 vols., México D.F.: Editorial Pormoca, 1965); and Pablo Casanova "La Sociedad Plural" in *La Democracia en México* (México D.F.: ERA, 1965).

28. On the 1994 Chiapas civil strife, see James D. Cockcroft, *Mexico's Hope: An Encounter with Politics and History* (New York: Monthly Review Press, 1998); and also the pertinent parts of Patrisia Gonzáles, *The Mud People: Chronicles, Testimonies and Remembrances* (San José, CA: Chusma House, 2003).

29. Guillermo Bonfil Batalla, *México Profundo* (Austin: University of Texas Press, 1996). For a specifying and updating as well as examining transborder relations in *México Profundo*, see Patrisia Gonzáles, *The Mud People: Chronicles, Testimonies and Remembrances* (San José, CA: Chusma House, 2003). For a recent examination of Indigenous as transborder immigrants, see Jonathan Fox and Gaspar Rivera-Salgado, *Indigenous Mexican Migrants in the United States* (Center for U.S.-Mexico Studies, UCSD, 2004).

30. For considerations of integral narratives and interpretation, see James H. Merrell, "Some Thoughts on Colonial Historians and American Indians," *William and Mary Quarterly*, 3rd Ser., 46 (1989); Daniel K. Richter, "Whose Indian History?" ibid., 50 (1993); Frederick E. Hoxie, *The Indians Versus the Textbooks: Is There Any Way Out?* (Chicago, 1984); F. E. Hoxie, "The Problems of Indian History," *Social Science Journal*, 25 (1988); and Francis Jennings, *The Invasion of America: Indians, Colonialism, and the Cant of Conquest* (New York: W. W. Norton, 1976). A pioneering integrative historical study is Roxanne Dunbar-Ortiz, *Roots of Resistance, Land Tenure in New Mexico, 1680-1980* (Los Angeles: CSRC/AISC, UCLA, 1980). Some recent materials on Native Americans and others are Jack Forbes, *Africans and Native Americans: The Language of Race and the Evolution of Red-Black People* (Urbana: University of Illinois Press, 1995); Richard White, *The Roots of Dependency: Subsistence, Environment and Social Change Among the Choctows, Pawnees and Navajo* (Lincoln: University of Nebraska Press, 1983); and *The Middle Ground: Indians, Empires and Republics in the Great Lakes Region 1650-1815* (Cambridge: Cambridge University Press, 1991). A readable narrative is David Hurst Thomas, et al., *The Native Americans: An Illustrated History* (Atlanta: Turner Publishing, 1993). Conventional Western historiography depended on the Turner thesis, which is of course a paradigm of expansionism; see Frederick Jackson Turner, *The Significance of the Frontier in American History* (ed. Harold P. Simonson, New York: Frederick Unger, 1963).

31. On Native Americans and the early colonists of the United States, see Russell Bourne, *The Red King's Rebellion: Racial Politics in New England 1675-1678* (London: Oxford University Press, 1990); and Neal Salisbury, *Manitou and Providence: Indians, Europeans, and the Making of New England, 1500-1643* (London: Oxford University Press, 1982); and for a neo-conservative view of Native Americans as crucial first enemy, see David Horowitz, *The First Frontier, The Indian Wars and America's Origins, 1607-1776* (Simon and Schuster, 1978).

32. For Thomas Jefferson's views, see Anthony F. C. Wallace, *Jefferson and the Indians: The Tragic Fate of the First Americans* (Cambridge: Harvard University Press, 1999). The historian David Weber in several publications describes the initial encounters between Spanish speakers and English speakers, see his *The Spanish Frontier in North America* (Yale University Press, 1992). See also Landon Y.

Jones, *William Clark and the Shaping of the West* (New York: Hill and Wang, 2004). The literature on Lewis and Clark does not abate, and associations of "Western" historians regularly host panels and panelists on the subject. For a report of Native Americans confronting Lewis and Clark re-enactors, see *Navajo Times* (September 23, 2002) "Delegation Confronts Lewis and Clark Re-enactors."

33. Tzvetan Todorov, *The Conquest of America: The Question of the Other* (New York: Harper Perennial, 1984). A review in the *American Historical Review,* Vol. 91 (1986) compliments the book for its interpretive and methodological insights. A new edition appeared in 1999. Todorov is of course an example of recently culturally premised literature on encounters. For the considerable English language literature on encounters, see James Axtell, "Columbian Encounters, 1992-1995," *William and Mary Quarterly,* 3rd Ser., 52, (1995). For Larry McMurtry, see *In a Narrow Grave, Essays on Texas* (New York: Simon and Schuster, 1968); and *Sacagawea's Nickname, Essays on the American West* (New York: New York Review of Books, 2004).

34. Dee Brown, *Bury My Heart at Wounded Knee, An Indian History of the American West* (original 1971, New York: Vintage, 1991); Vine Deloria, *We Talk, You Listen: New Tribes, New Turf* (New York: MacMillan, 1970); and *Custer Died for Your Sins* (University of Oklahoma Press, 1988). For a more recent perspective see Troy R. Johnson, et al., eds., *American Indian Activism* (University of Illinois Press, 1997); and M. Annette Jaimes, *The State of Native America* (South End Press, 1992).

35. On the Native Americans and early United States administrations, see Reginald Horsman, *Expansion and American Indian Policy, 1783-1812* (Reprint ed., Norman: University of Oklahoma Press, 1992); R. Douglas Hurt, *The Indian Frontier, 1763-1846* (Albuquerque: University of New Mexico Press, 2002); Anthony F. C. Wallace, *Jefferson and the Indians: The Tragic Fate of the First Americans* (Cambridge: Harvard University Press, 1999); Michael Paul Rogin, *Fathers and Children, Andrew Jackson and the Subjugation of the American Indian* (Alfred A. Knopf, 1975); and Loring

Benson Priest, *Uncle Sam's Stepchildren: The Reformation of United States Indian Policy 1865-1887* (Reprint edition, Lincoln: University of Nebraska Press, 1969).

36. On the mid and later nineteenth century United States administrations, see Robert Utley, *The Indian Frontier of the American West, 1846-1890* (Albuquerque: University of New Mexico Press, 1984); and D. S. Otis, ed., *The Dawes Act and the Allotment of Indian Lands* (Norman: University of Oklahoma Press, 1973). A basic reference is Francis Paul Prucha, ed., *Documents of United States Indian Policy* (University of Nebraska Press, 1990).

37. On Native Americans and twentieth century administrations, see Alvin M. Josephy Jr., *Now That The Buffalo's Gone* (University of Oklahoma Press, 1985); Graham D. Taylor, *The New Deal and American Indian Tribalism: The Administration of the Indian Reorganization Act, 1934-45* (Lincoln: University of Nebraska Press, 1980); and George Pierre Castile, *To Show Heart: Native American Self-Determination and Federal Indian Policy, 1960-1975* (Tucson: University of Arizona Press, 1998).

38. On the Ronald Reagan press conference at Moscow State University, May 31, 1988, see *New York Times* (June, 1988). As to the state of respect for such foundational human prerogatives such as respect for the dead and religious freedom for Native Americans two hundred years after U.S. independence, see Kathleen S. Fine-Dare, *Grave Injustice* (University of Nebraska Press, 2002); and John T. Noonan and Edward McGlynn Gaffney, *Religious Freedom* (New York: Foundation Press, 2001).

39. For Native Americans in the late twentieth century, see Fergus M. Bordewich, *Killing the White Man's Indian: Reinventing Native Americans at the End of the Twentieth Century* (New York: Doubleday, 1996); Jack Utter, *American Indians: Answers to Today's Questions* (2nd ed., Norman: University of Oklahoma Press, 2001); David Wilkins, *American Indian Politics and the American Political System* (Lanham, MD: Rowland and Littlefield, 2002); Leslie Marmon Silko, *Yellow Woman and a Beauty of the Spirit: Essays on*

Native American Life Today (New York: Simon and Schuster, 1996); and Nancy Shoemaker, *American Indian Population Recovery in the Twentieth Century* (University of New Mexico Press, 1999). See also Philip Jenkins, *Dream Catchers, How Mainstream America Discovered Native Spirituality* (Oxford University Press, 2004).

40. The Native American press and museum advocates welcome the realization of the long sought and obviously long overdue recognition of Native American historical and contemporary presence. See *Navajo Times* (September 23, 2004). For some views by the Native Americans, see *Washington Post* (September 22, 2004), "On the Mall: A Feast for the Eyes." For a skeptical view, see Marc Fisher, "Indian Museum's Appeal, Sadly, Only Skin Deep," *Washington Post* (September 21, 2004). For a timely work on the representation of Native Americans by an author who writes on both museums and Native Americans, see Steven Conn, *History's Shadow: Native Americans and Historical Consciousness in the Nineteenth Century* (Chicago: University of Chicago Press, 2004).

The above Mexica/Aztec image of the reptile superimposed on the Wind God symbolizes man pierced by the luminous arrow of consciousness. This symbol was taken from the Codex Borgia as represented in the book *Burning Water: Thought and Religion in Ancient Mexico* by Laurette Séjourné.

PART TWO:

STALKING WORDS

"A thousand shimmers,
across rivers and lakes
springs a single moon."
JGQ

"Humility,
Perseverence,
Respect, Honor,
Love, Sacrifice,
Truth, Compassion,
Bravery, Fortitude
Generosity, Wisdom"
The Lakota Way

STALKING WORDS
FOLLOWING THE TRACTS OF HERITAGE:
THEORIZING INDIGENITUDE(S) BEYOND NATIVISM

 Subject

North American Indigenitude – the quality of being Indigenous – is the heritage of persons of Native American/Amerindian ancestry, the descendents of those living in North America prior to 1500. This Indigenitude is a social being reality as well as a deeply historical material and ideational complex. The facts are broadly referenced in diverse materials, although specific data is minimally available. This essay explores the philosophical possibilities of constructing a theory of Indigenitude, a task undertaken respectful of autonomous Native American heritages and valid scholarships.[1] The task involves several stages: theorizing; deconstructing the elements of a possible theory; and outlining a coherent schema about world view, social organization, ethics, and aesthetics. The end achievement is a preliminary summary exposition on Indigenist cosmology (world and society), Indigenist citizenship (equality and autonomy), and Indigenist ethics (values and aesthetics). The exposition, which bridges the historical with the contemporary, consists of assertions on culture, education, aesthetics, and civics. Also presented are negations of mistaken views that appear in the colonial scholarly literature and that inform all too many political, cultural, and aesthetic expressions. Currently there exists no other printed articulation of a theoretical framework of Indigenitude as a contemporary sociocultural set of beliefs.

Studying the intellectual heritage of Native Americans expresses appreciation of a particular legacy and deepens our understanding of other human societies.[2] Certainly, the study of Indigenitude may provide an overarching schema for curricular design and classroom use. Ultimately, the project of theorizing vis-à-vis the Indigenous is an answer to false colonialist epistemology, which has long denied autonomy to the Indigenous in intellectual matters – intellectual sovereignty. Materials include, but are not limited to, past and contemporary Indígena-Native American heritage records; representations and historiographical materials in Indigenous languages; and Spanish and English language materials pertaining either to Mexico or the United States. Theorizing is possible because Indigeneity, Indian being, is both historical and contemporary.

Indigenitude in practice stresses persons and peoples – real social relations whose postulates are learned through pedagogy. Education, in turn, offers critiques and prescriptions for social relations. A complex dialectic thus exists between the material and the ideal. For the purpose of this argument, the emphasis is on the increasingly referenced Native American intellectual compendium. Prioritized is information that underscores Indigenous social interactions throughout North America, irrespective of group distinctions and state borders. Indigenism transcends birthplace and group identification; it is an intellectual constellation of premises and priorities, the distinguishing values and beliefs of individuals and groups: in short, an ethos.

This presentation is decidedly not an academic integration of the immense variety of Indigenous intellectual heritages per se; or a justification along so-called Western European intellectual lines; or an attempt merely to eulogize or mystify. Certainly, no justification is asked, and no idealistic gilding required. The fact is that in the past many colonialistically focused scholars knew very little pertinent to the Indigenous intellectual heritage. Further knowledge still requires time. We are here to be critical not just of others, but of self. This will include a consideration of repudiations of what is presented herein.

To begin with, the term "Indigenitude" is problematic in and of itself, as are so many Western language terms applied to the Indigenous. We question whether the term is adequate or appropriate, or even equitably translatable among several languages. For example, the English term Indigenitude is likely to be confused with the older usage of the Spanish term "indigenismo," which refers to early and mid-twentieth century trends centered on applied government social policies or arts inspirational motifs in the republic of Mexico. This essay's assertion of Indigenitude re-appropriates and re-configures this and other Indigenous-related terms from passive manipulation to a proactive stance. To be sure, the term Indigenitude is no more or less problematic than are several other terms such as "Indian," "Native," "Amerindian," "Primal," "Indigeneity," or "Indigenism," to name only a few. In this essay, the usage of the term "Indigenism" pertains to the thoughts and ideas of the pro-Indigenistas of the late 20th century in both the United States and Mexico who upheld the social welfare and intellectual heritage of the Indigenous as high personal and public values. Indigenism is not per se "anti" anyone or any entity; Indigenism is a multifaceted heritage independent of a sponsoring or sustaining state apparatus(es).

As constant dwellers of the land, the Indigenous are foundational and fundamental to the construction of those who now dominate the Americas.[3] Emphatically we say, Indigenous have made modern Americans possible. Being Mestizo or hybrid is Indigenously premised; so is being a dominator. More to the point, entire social networks of Indigenous peoples persist and even thrive across North America, and Indigenous-African-Mestizo/Caucasian relations are salient aspects of urban and rural communities alike. Unfortunately, the contemporary academic world often reduces the complexities of Indigenous relations to sociological clichés or commentaries on the exotic; the mythic to esoteric word game trivia; and Native American Studies to an academic afterthought (while other "studies" are touted). Even in some ostensibly "Americas" history courses, today's Indigenous are portrayed as a people without history, not because they are not granted a past, but because arguably they do not have a future. By contrast, within their own internal discourses, Indigenous persist in examining colonial and post-colonial Indigenous dominations and the role of these dominations in the becoming of other minorities. Social and critical interests drive these analytical questionings.

Theories about Indigenism stem from the convergence of several developments: the growth of some Indigenous populations; the civic dynamism of Indigenous peoples; the upsurge in academic studies on Indigenous; and the increasing interest that the Indigenous are showing in their own aesthetic, philosophical, and spiritual traditions. Moreover, today's Indigenous organize and represent themselves, thus energizing social relations and ideological discourse. Indigenous migrants from Mexico and Central America are increasing in numbers and dispersions within the U.S. where they are retaining many of their cultural traditions and beliefs. In Mexico, meanwhile, the Indigenous are mobilizing in many ways and places. In short, Indigenous continue to make history; they are a presence that is at once past, present, and future.

 Queries: "Venimos a Contradecir"

In our late-modern world, we know that extant Indigenous historical materials support injunctions to question, to remember, to theorize. Indigenous voices recorded in the *Códice Matritense* (sixteenth century) pose many of the questions central to the purpose of this essay. One passage of the document asks: "What will be our standard? What will be our measure? What will be our pattern? From where should we begin? What will be our torch, our light?"[4] These questions invite a variety of theoretical perspectives and an empirical substantiveness. The voices in the *Crónica Mexicayotl* (sixteenth century) likewise enjoin us to historicize: "Never will the legacy be lost, never will it be forgotten, that which they came to do, that which they came to record in their paintings: their renown, their history, their memory. Thus in the future never will the legacy perish, never will it be forgotten, always we will treasure it, we, their children, their grandchildren, brothers, sisters, great-grandchildren, great-great-grandchildren, descendants, we who carry their blood and their color, we will tell it, we will pass it on to those who do not yet live, who are to be born, the children of the Mexicans, the children of the Tenochcans."[5] This statement communicates the charge of responsibility for transmitting the heritage. To be sure, the transmittal is subject to endangerment.

This exploration is grounded in primary sources, aesthetic as well as historiographical, and audio and visual materials from a variety of locations. In some cases, unfortunately, the data expresses contradictions, or repeats false stereotypes or essentialized homogenizations that need revision – for example, supposed concepts of "dualism," "time," "history" and so forth. Central questions address the creation and continuation of the Indigenous within North American socio-cultural relationships and motifs, and the contradictions implied by this continuation. We also consider the current global tendencies pertaining to the Indigenous. The documentary coverage spans a wide variety of sources, particularly those representing "voice" and "thought," and focuses on Indigenous historical material as well as contemporary recycling of this material in cultural communities throughout North America. Such recycling occurs with increasing frequency across borders, and the Mexican-United States community is but one site where individuals are calling for further examination of their Indigenous heritage. Indigenism flies its own theoretical flag, being inherently extra-Western and countering the Eurocentric diffusionism fundamental to contemporary academic social thought, whether conservative or progressive.[6]

Theorizing is coherent, informed questioning, questioning that leads to hypothetical conceptualization(s). Certain questions arise as we endeavor to construct our paradigm. How is the individual voice recognized? What are the contextual historical societies? How is the historicity of group memberships reflected in identities? How will they be represented? What is to be remembered, who cannot be forgotten? How is domination referenced – materially, intellectually and socially? We may also ask: How do dominators constrain yet motivate? We prioritize Indigenous persons and voices and prefer that these be our foundation, inspired by age-sanctioned injunctions. Always, importantly, we confront how Indigenous, speaking as "we," construct their reality. We follow cues indicating how the Indigenous have envisioned the cosmos and the entirety of human relations, and how this historicity is affirmed in evolving ways by Indigenous individuals and groups. Whether global or local, formal or informal, Indigenous tendencies raise the problematics of an imagined future; as much has changed in the past, much can change in the future.

The description of social organization and the calibration of a chronology are important but distinct tasks. Both are expressions of culture; and culture is more than traits or norms, more than a timeline. This human stuff is quite specific, yet also elusive and contradictory. Cultures are complex systems made up of human behaviors neither random nor homogenous, but more or less adaptive by individuals. Thus, in addition to inspecting cultural materials, mega-cultural continuities must be contextualized. Native local spacial sites, cultural-regional dimensions, and the links between present and past are central to theorizing. Reflections on these allow for hypothesis, which in turn effects theory. Theorizing involves conjecture and inferences, as well as attention to specifics that lead to mid-range deductions.

What theory offers, above all, is testable statements that tell a story. Collectively these statements form a possible narrative explanation for history. Theorizing does not mean inspecting history as an absolute record of the past; nor does theorizing mean positing or rationalizing a single tunneled perception of the past. All theories are, in fact, false when understood as realities. On the other hand, theories are arguably true – or at least possessed of their own reality – when viewed as interpretations. Theorizing occurs in varied contexts: the context of the lived experience; the context of the perceptions of these experiences; and the context of the theoretical tools themselves. To draw the map and even to use the map is not necessarily to make the journey. Indeed, the journey inevitably leads to a redrawing of the map. The task of theorizing likewise involves prioritizing demanding choices and possibilities.

Herein is a hypothesis: Being Indigenous is the conscious experience of Native descent and lived culture historically situated in the Americas; of a historical memory related to awareness of a Native group membership; and of an ethos that recognizes exploitation and discrimination, past, present and future. Indigenism involves understanding the convergence of history and the present, and gaining from this understanding a motivation to change the present.[7] Ultimately, Indigenism is a matter of the heart whereby kinship, accountability, and responsibility are felt and acted upon for the common good. As Indigenous peoples contest domination, discrimination, and exploitation, their will to survive is sustained by an ethos of selflessness and generosity. The altruism is demanding.

To theorize about Indigenism entails several endeavors: 1) indicating multiple contexts; 2) identifying basic tracts toward generalizing; and 3) outlining basic elements of a general paradigm. This paradigm, a hypothetical construct for Indigenism, includes philosophical constructions important to human life: cosmology, human nature, society; and the analytical constructions important to social change: diagnosis, ideology, and critique. To be sure, theorizing Indigenism is philosophically and analytically problematic since it involves generalizations that transcend specifics and thus invariably suffer from some flaw related to data, logic, imagination, or language. Nonetheless, Indigenism is as real as the Indigenous themselves.

 Multiple Contexts: The Historical and the Perceptual

The cues for theorizing about Indigenism appear in the geographical and historical context.[8] The heuristic or conceptual framework for Indigenous Theory is hemispheric, not limited by ethnicity or region, by one group or time. From an Indigenous perspective, North America is a single historical zone with shared cultural influences and trends. Within this zone are areas of Indigenous demographic concentration, e.g., in Mesoamerica (southern North America), which have exerted a broad and seminal cultural influence on all of North America. To consider "the Native American/Amerindian societies" requires examining site-specific original social formations and historical developments. The historical context of North American Indigenism encompasses transforming economies and societies from early human times to the present. Early human habitation may date from 10,000 years ago to perhaps three times that estimate. Arguably the earliest humans in North America shared similar economies, language, technology, and cultural practices which involved hunters, small bands, leadership, and animistic beliefs. A unique human culture arises. Once agriculture ensues, change quickens. The three millennia B.C.E. (before the common era) represent an important formative epoch in relation to civilizational characteristics with tremendous growth, development, and diversification. Natives constructed diverse societies in Mesoamerica, resulting in outstanding cultural developments. Native American mores and beliefs were no less developed than that of other peoples across the globe at that time, and in some expressions, the Yucatan Maya for example, quite sophisticated.

Although biased accounts say otherwise, for Native Americans there was no simple externally impelled "emergence" and no rude internal "decline." Despite academic condescension about "prehistory" and "ethnographic" presence, Indigenous have existed historically and continue to exist. In the late fifteenth century, Europeans invaded North America; autonomous Indigenous development nearly ended as a result.[9] European colonialism meant political rule, social domination, economic exploitation, and ideological oppression – in short, near-total hegemony. Colonialist practices relegated the Indigenous to marginal "participants" and appropriated Indigenous lands as "the West." Thus did the Indigenous arrive into the world affairs of the modern era, defined by Europeans as adjuncts and tributaries. Since the European encounter, Indigenous humans and geographies have been continuously dominated by large foreign states and their economic initiatives. The "present" that stems from these encounters is multiple: it is Indigenitude preserved by various Indigenous individuals.

From 1500 to 1800, Indigenous adaptations were irrevocable responses to direct rule by Europeans.[10] During these 300 years, tremendous dislocations and adjustments occurred across the length and breadth of North America. Nothing less than the losses of land, sovereignty, science, and religion occurred amidst continual – not episodic – genocide. The Indigenous survived despite tremendous losses. In the late eighteenth and early nineteenth centuries, interactions intensified among Indigenous peoples, and "minority" Indian populations persisted throughout North America. Meanwhile, descendants of so-called settler "Americans" maintained local domination and moved to autonomize themselves not just from British and Iberian rule, but from the economic and intellectual influence of European powers.

As the histories of the United States and Mexico developed, Indian histories developed as well. During the nineteenth century, Indian presence could be found in all spaces of present-day Mexico and the United States, and migration was commonplace. An Indigenous from central Mexico moved northward to form, with others, Spanish-speaking Mestizo settlements in what is now the Southwest United States. Subsequently, in the nineteenth century, a few Indigenous from the United States, perhaps speaking Spanish or English in addition to their native language(s), moved into the Mexican republic south of the Rio Bravo. Since then, Spanish and non-Spanish-speaking Indigenous have constituted a significant part of Mexican migration to the United States, and persons of Indigenous descent from central Mexico are conspicuous in Mexican-American U.S. Southwest communities. Not only do the United States, Mexico, and Canada have Indigenous peoples associated with their claimed territories, these also are legal-political sites from which Indigenous have moved, across them and among them. For example, there are persons from Indigenous groups once from Mexico residing in Canada. There are descendants of Zapotecs talking to descendants of Iroquois, whether in the northeast United States, or on its borderlands with Canada. Moreover, all three large national states have transient Indigenous peoples within their borders. Although borders are sometimes demarcated with force, native language, English and Spanish-speaking Native Americans manage to meet each other and "others" across borders – all carrying history and history's images with them.

Across North America after the arrival of ostensible statehood and/or modernity, harsh colonialistic practices blended with modern post-colonialism. As they have for centuries, Westerners operate solely from the point of view of their economic and political interests. At one time such behavior was referred to as colonial, today it manifests as globalization. Masquerading as progress, its objectives are profit and power. Elites from Europe and the United States drive the globalization, which creates and expands and then erases its extensions. Just as colonialistic narratives once pejoratized Indigenous thought and culture, contemporary economic discourse overlooks or discounts Indigenous responses to globalistic travesties.

The globalistic enterprise has not just impacted the social, economic, and political life of Indigenous, it has, inevitably, shaped their perceptions as well.[11] The sum is this: with discrimination and exploitation came the need to justify; the West colonized and rationalized concurrently.[12] Indigenous thus live in a particularly European or Western constructed ideological world. The consequences of this reality are palpable. Yet to arrive at a material and ideological synthesizing definition for colonialism, subalternity, and post-colonialism is problematic. Colonizers and colonialists are still here. There is in colonialistic representations in several media a veiling of realities, a sanctioned distortion.[13] Moreover, from the total there is a touted canon, the best of the worst. The authority of this canon is unquestioned and its arguments go largely uncritiqued. While the canon inspires resistance and insurgencies among some Indigenous, it also generates continual ambiguities. In most specific cases these problematics are linked to psychological and intellectual insecurities and real oppressions. For the Indigenous, "mestizaje hybridity," the initiating biology of colonialism, is burdensome. This mezcla is no less ambiguous and contested than the other multiple legacies of colonial occupation. Yet mestizaje must be contested and appropriated. The abstract representations and designations assigned to colonial history, after all, have real and ongoing power relations at their core.

Consistently, social analysis of the Indigenous in the social sciences and humanities is overwhelmingly communicated in racial terms.[14] In the Americas, derogatory racial referents appeared first in reference to the Indigenous: "Indio" and "india" are racial constructs that deny peoplehood. Post-European racialized contexts are of course ubiquitous today. Indigenous suffer racism from a variety of sources; indeed, "indio/a" is a subject of multiple denials and a label of a conglomerate of racisms. Too often "indio/a-indian" materials in both Spanish and English obfuscate the core "racist" denotation of these terms with clichéd rationalizations about levels of development, or optional social choices, or the anthropological in contrast to the biological. They deny Indigenous equality. Today, racialisms are veiled and often denied; as such they are more pernicious than ever.

The fact is that "race" and racialization are colonial residues; in the deep past, "race" had yet to be constructed.[15] We know, sometimes without overtly admitting it, that Indigeneity is not reducible to race – that "Indian" represents a reality and a challenge that far transcends race. "Race," "ethnicity," "tribe," "colonialization," "nationality," "identity," "Indian," or "Indio/a," and "Mestizo/a" are all loaded words. These terms are cultural, racial, and social homogenizations, as well as intrusive, politicized constructs. Yes, the definition of "race," as applied to Indigenous, continues to evolve, but its implications and repercussions remain. To be sure, progressive commentators seldom take on the issue of racism as it pertains to the Indigenous; the "race" of the Indigenous is brushed away along with their history.

Historically, Indigenous possess their own uniquely elaborated referents for understanding themselves and the world.[16] Their responses transcend Eurocentric manipulations. Racialized classifications, constructions, and exclusions are the instruments of those who hold power, not the rational responses of those discriminated against. Suspect biological racial theories and ersatz states – European constructs – are not adequate for Indigenous ideals. The Indigenous themselves, define themselves, define their personhood.

 ## Key Tracts: Learning, Thinking, Language, Space and Science

Indigenous knowing, or epistemology, is an irreducible foundation of personhood. Indigenous learning results from observation of and experimentation upon nature; and from calculated reflection upon history. These learning processes are inspired by and appropriate to people of certain shared experiences and locales, and they spring from a deep appreciation of change as well as continuity. To know Indigenous is to know and embrace change. Here are four

changes understood by Indigenous: 1) The Indigenous are historically determined first by Indigenous choices, later by choices of others; 2) An Indigenous social order once prevailed, later came an
imposed and discriminatory one, racialized and/or segregated; 3)
A variety of Indigenous economic practices once sustained Indigenous groups, later Indigenous are economically expropriated and/
or exploited as part of a general economic worldwide order; and 4)
Indigenous once engaged in varied autonomous or internally negotiated governances, later Indigenous are politically dominated and/
or disenfranchised peoples who share a set of cultural conditions.
Each of these changes is a historical inheritance that impacts the
daily lives of individuals.

Although the world is continually subject to change, Indigenous understand it to be generally comprehensible through communication and inquiry.[17] Observations, reasoning, language, and
space are integral to Nativist intellectual reflection. Indigenous reflections are premised on the interrelatedness of phenomena, the es-
sentiality of truth, and the importance of questions, unasked as well
as asked. These questions may be especially pertinent to nature, of
which Indigenous see themselves as members. Indeed, Indigenous
perception is always contextualized. There is a quality of equanim-
ity in Indigenous thinking akin to relativism but more substantive,
because humanist tolerance is accompanied by tough ethics.

There are three major questions in Indigenous learning: 1)
What is my place in the world? 2) What is the place of my surround-
ings in the cosmos? 3) What is the right path to follow in order to
fulfill my responsibilities as a member of the cosmos? Indigenous
approach these questions with premised argumentation as well
as purposeful observation: it is a way of thinking that is learned
through exemplification. This thinking synthesizes induction and
deduction; it stresses the particular. Above all, Indigenous thinking
is flexible: objective and subjective, logical and extra-logical. For
example, among some groups, counting evolved into mathematics,
i.e., the use of calculations to imagine and thus understand beyond
counting items or phenomena within the several time frameworks
of the past, present, and future. Yet in addition to curvilinear and
extra-sequential thinking, linear thinking is often employed. Linearity is considered neither an ideological virtue nor an argumenta-

tive weakness, it is simply one of many mental modes employed in thinking about time.

Stereotypical notions about so-called "Indian Time" are reductionist and racist, i.e., Indians cannot tell time. Indigenous understand time as having both subjective and objective meanings and complex/multiple applications.[18] Questions such as "Who is counting time?" "Through whose eyes?" and "Why is time being counted?" are distinct considerations. In these matters the Indigenous address contentious historical interpretations and multifaceted cultural practices. The question of a linear starting point is not one of specific inclusion or exclusion, but rather that all possible time(s) is(are) included from all possible perspectives from the earliest to the most recent, from the most specific to the most general. The Indigenous are in step with their own timing; yet they are neither synchronically nor diachronically out of step with time as it is commonly understood among Europeans. Clearly, Native American historical calendaring includes colonization, an encounter that occurred quite specifically in regard to calendar conditions, content, and consequences. Indigenous post-occupation materials underscore how Mesoamerican people were affected not only by specific colonial dictates, but also by generalized material and ideological developments during the nineteenth century and beyond. They certainly consider themselves a part of twentieth and twenty-first century global changes. Colonialization neither begins nor ends in these periods; yet the beginning of its end can be established by thoughts and actions by and on behalf of the Indigenous in the present moment.

Space, like time, has more consciously constructed aspects for Indigenous than may be apparent at first glance.[19] Space is not just terrain and distance, space is also history and memory; there is also the space of imagination. Space, in short, is contexualized, and spatial identifications are as varied as the people themselves. It can be literal or figurative. Space may be a circle, but the circle is movable. In North America, Indigenous traversed all terrains physically long ago, and these places can be mentally revisited through memory and ritual. All aspects of North American land and water are known, identified, and characterized. Land and water features in turn are sources of meditation and inspiration. The understanding of space is not limited to geography on a supra-individual scale; in fact, the identification may be quite personal. In the pedagogical, topographical, and perhaps psychological sense, there are no unknown, unexplored terrains – though in the spiritual sense, there may be.

Historical memoir, one important form of communication, is possible through vocal language, physical sign, graphic representation, and mental reasoning.[20] Historical and contemporary Indigenous subjects and actors are multilingual and multi-reasoning. Among Indigenous of the past and today, languages are many, complex, and ever-changing. Language and associated reasoning present challenges that reach beyond the formalities of multilingualism, bilingualism, or monolingual linearity. To be sure, present issues concerning language conceptualization, context and articulation are not adequately addressed in the literature by non-Indigenous on subject individuals or groups. Contrary to many monolinguals in the surrounding non-Indigenous society(ies), many Indigenous have historically spoken more than one language. Moreover, some Indigenous also communicate with various forms of nature and fellow nature sharers through reflection and meditation. Indeed, nature and animals, which are of course part of nature, can teach the observant and reflective human being.

 Three Further Tracts: Power, Epistemology and Practice

Power relations – projections as well as actualities – are important in Indigenous history and imaginings.[21] The evolution and transmittal of intellectual heritage is effected by human structures and stratifications. As colonialists constructed their system, power relations shifted not just between Indigenous and Europeans but among the Indigenous themselves. The power matrix allowed for differentiations between relatively disempowered Indigenous subjects and others who were more empowered. Such power disparities continue to exist among North America's Indigenous peoples, all of whom are confronted with the realities of a post-colonial universe.

Historically, Natives had governances adequate to their values and needs.[22] Indigenous civic thinking did not stress broad permanent overarching authority(ies), rather, it emphasized participation and fairness. Indigenous societies cohered via historical "laws" the accepted do's and don'ts established for the benefit of members and transmitted either orally or through explicit documentation. Upon European contact, however, Indigenous lived under coercion. Europeans did not inspire Native participatory democracy, they overthrew it. The laws applied to them were invader laws established according to invader logic. Inferior educational methods were also imposed. In the face of these realities, what can be said of politics or law that does not come full circle? Today, democracy – the direct participation of people in their own governance – hardly exists at a state level anywhere; yet ironically it is the ideal used to justify aggression and appropriation.

After a rich pre-European history of governance, pedagogy and epistemology, conditions have worsened for Indigenous. Since colonial rule, the transmission of Indigenous interests in knowledge, civics, and education have been superceded by undermining autonomous community self-development.[23] Although Indigenous people have long had multiple political relations among themselves, autonomy has become nearly impossible because of multiple intrusions. The various political relations among Indigenous, Mestizos, Mulattos, and Euros are multifaceted, but always weighted in favor of the Euros or hybrids in the spaces where Indigenous live.[24] As members of these, Mestizo or Euro sectors continue to impose hierarchies upon Indigenous. Discrimination and exploitation continue. Indigenous have been allowed little self-government despite much pretext to this effect.

While some modern schooling has been offered to some Indigenous, to date no pro-Indigenous education groups and efforts exist on a large sustained level autonomously. Pre-colonization schooling differed in many respects, most particularly in the transmission of Indigenous values. Nevertheless, Indigenous education was and is an inculcation of an ethos – a set of values and ethics that culminate in a strong heart and a wise character (corazón fuerte, rostro sabio). For many Indigenous, contemporary institutionalized schooling is by and large a non-Native set of practices inflicted on Indigenous to facilitate their participation in the larger society – on its terms.

Natives who demand schooling for and by natives are marginalized. To be sure, there are, here and there, some islands of education by and for Indigenous. Nevertheless, given the imposed limits on the spheres of governance and education, the biological, social, and civic survival of the Indigenous are quite striking.

Negative temporalities are reversible, not by reaction to them, but by a displacement in the game. Indigenous face disadvantages and restrictions not just in the realms of governance and education, but more insidiously, in the realm of academia, the regime of knowledge. Today, blood/skin attributes are the major criteria by which scholars identify Indigenous. In the past, however, issues of descent and geography were considered far more important in the identification and study of Indians. The issue is not an elusive correct ideology, but a politics of truth, changing the production of truth. Among some Indigenous, ethnicity, group membership, and cultural practices are all taken into account, encoded in a true heart whose sign is integrity. Among many Indigenous themselves, the defining truth is a historical and multifaceted ethos that can be identified, described, and valued (auto-valorizado), whose outlines can be imagined as an ethical paradigm.

 Paradigm in Six

I. Cosmology: Dimensions and Awarenesses

Cosmology is by definition temporally deep and materially inclusive.[25] The Indigenous cosmos includes all that has been and will be. Indigenous cosmology identifies the origins and design of the cosmos; explores humanity's place in the universe and its ultimate purpose; and offers a description of what constitutes matter and how matter is organized. Questions are addressed in a variety of ways: spiritually, religiously, philosophically, and empirically. That said, there are parts of the cosmos we do not know and will not know. Knowing and not knowing – both are part of the cosmos.

Within Indigenous cosmological thinking, certain points are salient. Creation is believed to emanate from the feminine, which is as all-encompassing as the cosmos itself, and can be perceived via reflection as well as observation. Indigenous cosmology assumes human beings to be aware of their inherent membership in the cosmos; there is no alienation to be speculated upon, no "I" separated from life. Nor is there any "evil" in the European sense. The cosmos may be constant, but it is not unchanging, and with change comes uniqueness of parts. An important symbol is the circle, which represents not some nostalgic notion of return, but rather a sense of autonomy, sufficiency, and harmony. The cosmos is accessible to humans via the beauty and wonder of nature; love and reverence for the cosmos is an essential part of being consciously Indigenous. Indigenous daringly take on the thought of non-existence. As for death: Death is considered part of a cycle in the cosmos; human matter and spirit – constituent parts integral to the universal whole – are transformed into water, earth, wind.[26]

Indigenous religious practices, both personal and social, consistently express respect and gratitude to the life force. Indigenous religion is a response to human ontological questioning, not an antecedent. To be human is to ask certain essential and unavoidable questions pertaining to individual and group identity. "Who am I?" leads to the question "Who are we?" These questions are asked, and answered, through a wide variety of rituals, most importantly shared narratives. Inanimate religious objects are revered as memory-charged representations and mediators. Memory-centered group practices generate positive social feeling through acts of solidarity and recollection. What is most important is sharing with others in the here and now. There are also a variety of social accompaniments; even rituals have their rituals. These are time-sanctioned prescribed acts where even the organizing is ritualized. Ritual is, among other things, the acknowledgement of human responsibility for the earth.

If religiosity is reverent action, spirituality is disciplined contemplation.[27] Indigenous cosmology is fundamentally spiritual. Spirituality can be understood as a reflection upon the great changes and great constancy of the cosmos. For the most part, spirituality is distinct from ritual, although rituality can assist in predisposing the individual to spirituality. Spiritual communication is absolutely private and not subject to queries about mode or content. Contemplation is, in other words, an individual process and as such separable from collective practices. Meditation is a route. Spirituality is possible because you are a person who is part of the cosmos who shares the life force of the universe with all other expressions of the life force. Personal vision, an aesthetic epiphany, a grasping of one's specific obligation in life, is a result of meditation upon one's life experience and discerning the possible choices for one's life direction. A vision thus offers practical guidance as well as an expression of the deepest longing for cosmological union and the momentary plenitude that results from glimpsing that possibility.

This experience, it must be said, is not a hebraic passport to an afterlife, though much affected by past and present borders. In Indigenous religiosity there is neither catechismal dogma, nor textual exclusivity, nor demanding structure, nor infallible authority; instead there is, most emphatically, personal responsibility and inner quietude – an acknowledgement of, and identification with, the life source. Indigenous religious observances and spiritual practices evolved over many centuries, whereas Christianity, often a state sponsored institution, was forced upon Indigenous in a single historical moment. Although some Indigenous have adapted some Christian beliefs and practices, these are adaptations rather than wholesale accommodation. This phenomenon suggests a distinct dissatisfaction with Christianity. Many Indigenous do not fully embrace this religion because it's inherent invidiousness is so often inconsistent with their own cultural matrix. The colonizers, for example, inculcated idolatry by their practices; Indigenous do not believe idols are gods. Most Christians are judged as not living Christian precepts. Christian doctrine notwithstanding, many Christians are more denominationally prejudiced than Indians who are likely to be tolerant in religious matters. Most Indians do not honor hypocrisy, many Christians do. Some Indigenous have viewed European Christian religion as the ideational form of colonial occupation and exploitation. In this view, Christian missionaries introduced innovations such as coercion, avarice, invidiousness and intolerance. Native religious practices and requirements differ from these. Moreover, such non-conformists argue, colonialists espoused the anti-humanist notion that a supernatural entity, i.e., the "devil," could explain away their malicious actions.

II. Human Nature

Being

Indigenous identify certain distinctly human traits, from which they in turn infer certain human assignments.[28] Human beings are considered unique individuals. Moreover, like the cosmos, human nature is essentially creative. It follows that part of one's duty as a human being is to express and share one's personal values and needs with other individuals and with the community at large. Such sharing of one's own personhood will help to ensure the survival and betterment of fellow humans. Sharing is an obligation to the self, to others, and indeed to the cosmos.

Sexuality

Gender, sex, and sexuality are expressions of personal identity as well as an integral part of the cosmos itself. Historical materials indicate that gender, sex, and sexuality have long played an important role in Indigenist social thought and religious culture. As an expression of the life force, sexuality consists of multiple strands, practices and expressions. Like a multi-strand braid, the multiple feminine and masculine elements intertwine to form a single solid entity that is also paradoxically multiple, a complex community. Within this paradigm, women and men occupy a variety of roles, from the most practical to the most dramatic and conceptual, and Indigenous find no contradiction among these roles. Yet, sexual roles inevitably involve power, and power acquisition is in a constant state of flux. Since the arrival of the Europeans, there have been striking changes in the female power matrix. Simple observation indicates that the burden of women's work has steadily increased, without a concommitant increase in status. There are, of course, obvious contradictions between, on the one hand, the understanding of the cosmos as emanating from the feminine, and on the other hand, the persistent subordination of women. This subordination manifests itself not just in daily events, but symbolically and rhetorically. For example, to describe women as engaged in "parallel" or "complementary" roles is a direct contradiction of the feminine centrality within Indigenism.

Personal

Consciousness is the major component of the Indigenous self – a critical awareness of what a person does and who she is socially. Although Indigenous thought clearly articulates conceptual dualisms, their ontology is premised on constantly shifting energies and transmutation. Consciousness thus operates in rhythm with and response to the whole body. There is no sharp dichotomy separating mind and body; bodily functionings are related to mental processes, which in turn are connected to soul energies that affect others as well as the self. There are two sources, or energies, of human thinking: primary (immediate and reactive), and secondary (deliberate and reflective). Up to a point, the energies are also the purposes. Wants, in other words, are not sharply separated from needs. Seemingly static states flow and blend; there are no irreconcilable differences or oppositions.

Social

Indigenous recognize that human nature has more than one dimension. The person expresses inner wonder; the person also acts outwardly. External behavior is guided by an immaterial spirit that interacts with mind and body; the human persona embraces both the physical constitution and the spiritual being. Individuals are thus responsible for their actions, good and bad alike; they are not subject to an imagined malignant influence that explains or excuses their behavior. The self, meanwhile, is empowered by the collective. Human singularity expresses its transcendence through the bonding with an other. This occurs in many ways via rational language and ritual, especially as it pertains to death. Death is a transition, perhaps a reintroduction to the larga vida, the long life. No less important than the obligation to live harmoniously with the family and society is an obligation to meet death in an appropriate way. A woman or man is most fortunate if circumstances allow her or him to prepare for death adequately and appropriately. Such preparation is perhaps the ultimate expressions of the desired union with the cosmos.

III. Human Society

Indigenous views are usually group-centered: the self identifies itself in relation to others; the self works and performs in relation to others. The Indigenous way of life is thus an expression of collectivity. The "we" is more important than the "I." As social relations are not historically fixed, Indigenous thoughts on self and society involve continually questioning.[29] Questions on group relations are answered with further questions, this time in the form of stories. These narratives address population dynamics, territoriality, economic production and social distribution, mega-authorities and micro-governances, group rights and respect for the individual, male and female equities, and group representations. Individuals depend on the group for their survival; the group in turn depends on intense bonds among its members. Bonds exist between men and women, women and women, men and men, and adults and children. A child is a gift to the parents, but also to the group. Women (who, by the way, are granted the latitude to abort) nurture children in the context of the community. Because children are so valued by the group, a premium is placed on disciplining them, cultivating an ethical attitude, and fostering a generous disposition. Above all, children are taught not to be lax in their duties – to themselves, their family, and especially the group as a whole. Society, after all, transcends the individual. "Survival" may be physical, but the conduit for survival is the spiritual. The cosmos is the destination of all humans.

Reflections on human nature naturally lead to the development of ethics. Such considerations are inextricably linked to an acknowledgment of free will. The individual chooses; the choice is both an expression of autonomy and an acceptance of responsibility. Human behavior may in part be biologically determined and species-specific; individuals are nonetheless accountable to themselves and to others. The realm of sexuality is particularly pertinent in this regard. Diverse sexualities are part of the natural order of the cosmos. There is latitude for sexual relations, but not for adultery: when partners have agreed to monogamy, this is what is expected. Personal behavior is embedded in communal ethics and norms. It should be noted that in Indigenous culture, these ethics and norms involve clear differentiations between recognized leadership and the general population. More service is expected of the leadership. There are certain human qualities that evoke the explanation of evolution – the gifts of a maestro for example. These gifts are considered essential for the construction, or reconstruction, of society. Indigenous leadership seeks to maintain, or to return to, a condition of economic and political equilibrium within the group. A good society is a just society for its members and, ultimately, one in which we live in rhythm and harmony within the cosmos.

IV. Aesthetics

Indigenous cultural life is an interactive process, one providing social as well as aesthetic pleasure.[30] Art exists for the group and the individual alike; there is communal as well as personal meaning. Indigenous aesthetics have three major concentrations: the cosmos; the meta-human, or heroic; and the quotidian human, i.e., the realistic. Historical memory serves as both a tool of cultural maintenance and a rationale for cultural change. Cultural practices and constructions emanate not just from cultural norms, but from basic human biology – which may or may not be suppressed by norms. Women are not just the transmitters of culture, they are also important practitioners of the arts. Of course, the cultural environment now involves a complex equation of influences: not just the influences of parents, teachers, and peers, but also corporations, advertising agencies, and media advocates.

The cultural depth and range of the Indigenous are amply demonstrated in the arts which offer not just individual representations, but entire systems of representation.[31] A single expression thus functions as part of a macro-statement of meanings. Public buildings, for example, assert a historical legacy as well as a claim on the future. Canals, monuments, dwelling places, and certainly religious sites all adhere to formal and careful designs – which are themselves mega-statements. Among Indigenous there are seldom "art-for-art's sake" articulations. Although quality is very much valued, the fundamental purpose of the artist is to convey specific meanings to the audience. Indeed, in Indigenous societies, art is very much a social phenomenon, particularly the arts of sound and motion, music and dance, thunderous drumming and choreographed silences. Symmetry, harmony, repose, horror, humor, cleverness, and profundity are all consciously valued aesthetics. Styles range from realism to symbolism, from abstraction to symbolism to petroglyphics. Flamboyant displays alternate with stillness and simplicity. There is no one representation of beauty and no one single endorsed form. Indigenous artistic practices can involve the face, the head, the body, and dress; the latter concerns not personal attractiveness, but rather creativity and communication. The range of Indigenous poetry and narratives is as impressive as its music and dance. All groups have imagined remarkable "stories" that amount to creative explanations of human nature. These so-called folklore, or myths, are literary creations that exemplify aesthetic ideals. Some narratives are particularly complex offering not just aesthetic enrichment, but also theological insights and philosophical and ethical pedagogy. Indigenous art is, in short, a dialogue on the role of humans in the cosmos.

Indigenous art is rooted in historical tradition, even as its value and purpose stems from its intrinsic breaking of tradition. The arts of Indigenous peoples evolved within relatively small groups, while sharing multiple influences from the arts of other peoples across the Americas. Multiple influences are visible in the arts of specific groups. Compared to the complex philosophical meanings of Aztec statuary or Hopi designs, Greek statues have simple descriptive meanings. Hopi and Navajo song lyrics are likewise more complex than the songs of the Greeks. To be sure, European-derived values, techniques, and forms have influenced Indigenous artists both past and present. More to the point is the continual evolution of Indigenous arts. The Indigenous value conceptual arts as well as representational forms; abstract and stylized modes are quite common. In Indigenous arts there is a sophisticated play between simplification and exaggeration, between the brutal and the absurd, that finds expression in caricature. Subjects are disguised or stylized nearly beyond recognition, lending a sense of powerful abstraction as well as playfulness. Such artistic self-confidence and technical achievement would test and supercede the seminal aesthetics of Aristotle because Indigenous aesthetics transgress and transcend the categories of paradox and contradiction, satire and tragedy.

V. Ethics

Indigenism, above all, involves the practice of social relations based on acknowledged human rights.[32] Rights can be expressed negatively or affirmatively: the right not to be killed, abused, exploited; alternatively, the right to be safe, recognized, and respected. More specifically, these rights manifest as the ability to maintain one's life and health; to safeguard one's family; to provide education for one's children; to work; and to pursue one's life purpose. To claim such rights is to accept responsibility. Indigenous believe that if you are benefitting by living, you have incurred responsibility by living. Respect for others is an end unto itself. The Indigenous see themselves as sharing a present and a future; the actions of each individual either add to or subtract from that future. One must strive for consciousness to live.

Indigenous are encouraged to act upon certain prescriptions vis-à-vis themselves and others.[33] Nine mandates express the cardinal meta-virtue of material and spiritual sharing: 1) personal responsibility: acting with consciousness; 2) high ideals of unselfishness and compassion: living ethics; 3) identifying injustices for what they are: practicing forthrightness; 4) generosity: proclaiming and upholding standards of goodness; 5) an ongoing presentation and narration of ideals: inculcating community values; 6) teaching people technology, manners and ideals: education and guidance; 7) being organized: promoting forms for a common ethical code; 8) beneficial economic practices: methods and tools for service and survival; and 9) recognition of the need for change in the social relations among women and men: tolerating and encouraging positive change.

VI. Diagnosis

Reflective Indigenous seek to identify the means for purposeful change to insure survival.[34] Breaking from tradition is a tradition unto itself. Critical Indigenous continually engage in a process of diagnosis that is both reflective and self-critical; they know persistence is adaptation. Analytical methods enable the identification of human defects and thus the improvement of individuals and social reform. Indigenous diagnosis, in short, is a critique of human realities in the service of possibilities. The "social ideal" is a prescription for how humans should live and how human society should operate. The standard is the cosmos.

Among conscious Indigenous there are two basic motivators: selfishness and love. Selfishness is perceived as the basic explanation underlying the errors or faults that so often occur. The core meaning of selfishness is self-indulgence, or personal gain at the expense of the welfare of others. Presumably, if you advocate certain forms of selfishness, or act on the assumption humans are selfish, you will have a society that reflects selfishness and is thus prone to imperfections and failures. Hence the Indigenous conclusion that selfishness is the fundamental flaw accounting for bad consequences. Conversely, Indigenous believe that if moral, that is, generous, behavior is expected and nourished, positive consequences will follow, along with a more nearly harmonious society. Indigenous morality is premised on the conviction that humans by and large are inclined to be generous. Love is perceived as the best corrective for human error. Love is defined as service and sacrifice for the immediate group, the concrete manifestation of the responsibility inherent in all life within the cosmos. A moral wrong results from a transgression of individual and group rights and usually involves some degree of premeditation. Such wrongdoing calls for atonement, and atonement is possible. Such atonement must occur publicly. In atonement the individual evidences their responsibility for their actions to the relevant family or group.

Indigenous believe that human needs are an objective fact and thus demand to be fulfilled. Critical self-examination by the self or the group serves not just as a means for correction or improvement, but also as a means of establishing standards. These standards are often, though not always, ethical, and they can be understood in a variety of ways. There exists, for example, a notion of good-sense ethics: an objective, non-religious code that derives morality from rationality alone. Another understanding of ethics derives from an awareness of subjugation and exploitation, and a desire to avoid or undo these wrongs in the future for the sake of human harmony. Conversely, ethics can be understood as a means of achieving the highest human potential. Indigenous thinkers generally endorse a combination of the benevolent and the practical. Human beings make choices as to the overall paths of their lives. Will they live ethically or not? Will they be self-defenders or nurturers?

Indigenous self-examinations amount to open questions on the human condition. How do you explain the harm and injustice that befalls so many people? Clearly, much of the suffering is due to irresponsible, abusive, or malicious actions by humans themselves. Indigenous materials offer several explanations for human suffering. In one scenario, harm results from accidents or arbitrary choices. The suffering may have a knowable but as yet unimagined cause; or it may occur for personal reasons. Another explanation for human suffering focuses on economic scarcity: i.e., nature and/or society does not provide enough for all human beings to live and reproduce. Population growth undermines economic well-being, producing new or unforeseen needs and scarcities. This situation tempts certain individuals toward radical selfishness, which in turn leads to manipulation, exploitation, or oppression. Yet another explanation cites unfair, arbitrary, or corrupt governance as a causal factor.

 Critique: A Summing

Theorizing on the Indigenous must be accompanied by intellectual critique.[35] Impartial, rational, philosophically guided assessments and challenges are not readily achieved. Let there be light on these reflections. Indigenous theory, it appears, can be questioned in three distinct ways. One way is to divorce the distant, formational past from the recent past – the twentieth century – by pointing to shifts in economics, governance, religion, and aesthetics. Undeniably, though, evidence indicates some historical continuities. Another way, seemingly more scholarly, would be to object to any ethnic-derived theorizing. Actually such a critique would undermine nearly all available social theories. A third, more provocative objection, would be to argue that the Indigenous is unknowable; those who know cannot speak and those who speak do not know, and thus no theorizing is possible. This argument, of course, wrongly presumes that there are no continuities between past and present and no knowledge whatsoever to be obtained from Indigenous individuals whether of yesterday or today. Indigenitude effectively does not exist in such a scenario. The ultimate purpose of theorizing may be the need to confront oppression strategically.

Beyond these three objections, an overarching critique would be to denounce theoretical generalizations as invalid. History, after all, is specific. This position would, of course, severely constrain the boundaries of knowledge. Only empirical data or the hermeneutics of anecdotes would qualify. A further critique would be to belittle interpretive findings as benign but ultimately valueless. This critique is along the lines of the argument that legal principles do not inform us on the workings of the courts. The fact is that principles do inform us, albeit not fully. Lastly, there is the critique that Indigenous theory does not offer substantive intellectual materials. A priori the subject, theorizing is dismissed. Some have encountered the faculty member who strenuously objects to positive interpretive statements on Indigenous heritage, kindly dismissing them as romanticisms, while at the same time embracing negative assertions supposedly offering up "truths" that justify colonialization. This person is dismissing Indigenous knowledge. In fact, all objections do.

Throughout academia, proponents and opponents use theorizing to defend "theory" itself, i.e., "theory" is a closed system. Arguments proceed as follows: 1) There are reasons [these are always logic statements], that is to say, intelligible connections between premises and conclusions couched in theoretical or/and practical reasoning; and 2) There are causes [these are often scientific statements] appealing to universal (always), or probable (maybe), regularities of nature that occur in particular contexts. The fact is that any given theory inevitably constitutes a response to other theories, thus implicitly reinforcing their reality. Theorizing on the Indigenous can lead far beyond Indigenous historical premises. Which theory gives face and body to life?

While analysts are not likely to solve all the ethnographic and conceptual challenges posed by Indigenous theory, the effort is intellectually worthwhile nevertheless. Indigenous theory is a contribution to the analysis of the human condition. Its paired problematic – the interaction of social relations and ideological reflections

– is a central idea in contemporary philosophy. Specifically, the problematics relate to discussions of free will within a world of seemingly as of yet uncontrollable forces. What is our universe, our world, our society, our future, and what are our beliefs in relation to these? A student of Indigenism may conclude: Everything, everything. Fine. Another response might be: Nothing, nothing. O.K. Everything and nothing lie within the cradle of change and bare what is new from what has been and is no more.

Not accidentally are legacies affirmed, denied, or reconstructed. This occurs in public life as well as academic studies and the realm of aesthetics. Obviously all subjects are not just empirical and theoretical, but also ideological, and the Indigenous are no exception. It is perhaps understandable that the Indigenous are exoticized and presented as mystical, given the persistent myth that they are unknowable. The fact is that all cultural constructions are as real and specific as the living narratives of our own lives. Cultural and civic citizenship proves transitional as the global supercedes the national; yet the local remains, is recreated and extended. There are no monolithic cultural containments in reference to the Indigenous. Culture and ethnicity were and remain central to people's lives; yet these social constructions are continually evolving, as they are everywhere.

Increasingly, Indigenous people speak loudly and organize publicly. Social analysts must now grapple with the realization that the objects of their analysis [i.e., persons] are also subjects with their own analysis to offer. Indigenous are more than ready to critically interrogate ethnographers and other academics; indeed, European-premised "authorities," their writings, their biases, and their politics are much questioned. The struggle of Indigenous women and men against oppression is the struggle for the survival of family memory, group autonomy, and individual dignity. Colonialization encouraged a forgetting and/or appropriating of the Indigenous past. For some Indigenous, narrating the past is a form of assertion.

Self-consciously, some Indigenous persons assert their personhood as individuals striving for freedom and joining other individuals seeking freedom. "Natives" are talking back, contradicting and reclaiming, refashioning history, insisting they are "themselves," neither the "other" nor the "exotic." Their life-affirming narratives and interpretive claims are far different from those that have shaped them as "others" in the narratives of domination yesterday, and of appropriation today. To begin to address these realities, we must listen to past voices and also pose questions to answer for our own times. The "we" is again being reconstructed, as is the history of yesterday, the history of today, and the history of tomorrow.

"For we are the ones we have been waiting for." Hopi prophecy

Endnotes

1. On the possible jumps and likely falls while theorizing, see Linda Tuhiwai Smith, *Decolonizing Methodologies* (Zed Books, 1999); Gregory Bateson, *Mind and Nature* (E. P. Dutton, 1979); Frantz Fanon, *The Wretched of the Earth* (Grover, 1968); and for a different critical stance on the world, see Rebecca Tsosie, "Surviving the War by Singing the Blues: The Contemporary Ethos of American Indian Political Poetry," *American Indian Culture and Research Journal*, Vol. 10 (1986). For the general history of native societies, see R. David Edmunds, et al., *The People: A History of Native America* (Houghton Mifflin, 2006); Colin G. Calloway, *First Peoples* (Bedford-St. Martins, 2004); and Alfredo López Austin and Leonardo López Luján, *El Pasado Indígena* (Fondo de Cultura Económica, 1996). For articulations on a range of historical-cultural issues by a contemporary Native American writer, see N. Scott Momaday, *The Man Made of Words* (St. Martin's Press, 1997). On false ways addressing the Indigenous, see Philip J. Deloria, *Playing Indian* (Yale University Press, 1998); and Shari M. Huhndorf, *Going Native* (Cornell University Press, 2001). Here no "tribal" history or religious rites are probed.

2. On antiquity, diversity and richness of historical cultures, see Richard E. W. Adams, *Prehistoric Mesoamerica* (University of Oklahoma Press, 1996); Richard E. Blanton, et al., *Ancient Mesoamerica: A Comparison of Change in Three Regions* (Cambridge University Press, 1981); Stuart J. Fiedel, *Prehistory of the Americas* (Cambridge University Press, 1987); Frances Joan Mathien and R. H. McGuire, eds., *Ripples in the Chichimec Sea: New Considerations in Southwestern-Mesoamerican Interactions* (Southern Illinois University Press, 1986); William A. Longacre, ed., *Reconstructing Prehistoric Pueblo Societies* (University of New Mexico Press, 1970); and Jacques Soustelle, *The Four Suns* (Grossman, 1970).

3. On recent and contemporary pan-Indian relations, see various organizational statements and also Roxanne Dunbar-Ortiz, *Indians of the Americas* (Zed Books, 1984); P. C. Smith and R. A. Warrior, *Like a Hurricane: The Indian Movement. . .* (New Press Publishers,

1996); Silvia Jaquelina Ramírez Romero, *La reconstruccíon de la identidad política* . . . (CNDPI, 2003); *Red Road Collective Newsletter*; Carlos Salomón, "Recent Impact of Transnational Indigenous Organizations in Mexico and the United States," in Irene Vásquez and D. O'Connor-Gómez, eds., *Proceedings of the Pacific Coast Council on Latin American Studies 2002-2003* (PCCLAS, 2005); and for background, Hazel W. Hertzberg, *The Search for an American Indian Identity: Modern Pan Indian Movements* (Syracuse University Press, 1971).

4. *Códice Matritense de la Real Academia de la Historia*, (editor Francisco del Paso y Troncoso, Fototipia de Hauser y Menet, 1906). On who speaks, consider Gayatri Chakravorty Spivak, "Can the Subaltern Speak?" in Cary Nelson and Lawrence Grossberg, eds., *Marxism and the Interpretation of Culture* (MacMillan, 1988); or the larger work, *In Other Worlds: Essays in Cultural Politics* (Routledge, 1988).

5. *Crónica Mexicayotl* [Fernando Alvarado Tezozomoc] (UNAM and INAH, 1949); and consult María del Carmen Nieva, *Mexi Kayotl*, (Editorial Orión [México D.F.], 1969). On historical longing and persistence, see Homi K. Bhabha, "Dissemination: Time, Narrative and the Margins of the Modern Nation," in Homi K. Bhabha, ed., *Nation and Narration* (Routledge, 1990). See also Elizabeth Hill Boone and Tom Cummins, eds., *Native Traditions in the Post Conquest World* (Dumbarton Oaks Research Library, 1998). For an interpretation of specific historical events and the communication of these, see Max Harris, "The Return of Moctezuma: Oaxaca's Danza de la Pluma" and "New Mexico's Danza de los Matachines," *The Drama Review*, Vol. 4 (Spring, 1997).

6. On the consequences and challenges responding to and surrounding racism, colonialism, and post-colonialism, see Francis Jennings, *The Invasion of America: Indians, Colonialism and the Cant of Conquest* (University of North Carolina Press, 1975); John E. Kicza, *Resilient Cultures, . . . 1500-1800* (Prentice-Hall 2003); Andrea Smith, *Conquest, Sexual Violence and American Indian Genocide* (South End Press, 2005); Guillermo Bonfil Batalla, *Et-*

nodesarrollo y Etnocidio (FLACSO, 1982); and Martha Menchaca, *Recovering History, Constructing Race* (University of Texas Press, 2001). For overarching critical commentary, see Kwame Anthony Appiah, "The Post Colonial and the Post Modern," in K. A. Appiah, *In My Father's House: Africa in the Philosophy of Culture* (Methuen, 1992). For social history, see Cynthia Radding, *Wandering Peoples: Colonialism, Ethnic Spaces, and Ecological Frontiers* (Duke University Press, 1997); and for an assessment of racism in expansion, see Rubin F. Weston, *Racism in U.S. Imperialism* (University of South Carolina Press, 1972).

7. On the studies of domination, subalternity and marginality, see the journals *Nepantla* (Duke University Press-U.S.); and *Subaltern Studies* (Oxford University Press-India); for such scholarship on the Americas, see Florencia Mallon, "The Promise and Dilemma of Subaltern Studies: Perspectives from Latin American History," *American Historical Review*, Vol. 99 (1994); for a discussion which invariably turns to Anglophone language, see Benita Parry, "The Scramble for Post Colonialism," in Chris Tiffin and Alan Lawson, eds., *De-Scribing Empire: Post-Colonialism and Textuality* (Routledge, 1994).

8. For deep and rich Mesoamerican cultural development, see Brian M. Fagan, *Ancient North America: The Archaeology of a Continent* (Thames and Hudson, London: 2000); Jacques Soustelle, *The Four Suns* (Grossman, 1970); and Miguel León-Portilla and Earl Shorris, eds., *In the Language of Kings* (Norton, 2001). For an examination of northern North America, see Olive Patricia Dickason, *Canada's First Nations* [2nd ed.] (Oxford University Press, 1997).

9. For Indigenous global encounters, participations and consequences, see Eric Wolf, *Sons of the Shaking Earth* (University of Chicago, 1959); Jayme A. Sokolow, *The Great Encounter* (M. E. Sharp, 2003); Norbert Elias, *The Civilizing Process*, Vol. 2, *State Formations and Civilization* (Pantheon Books, 1978); Leslie E. Bauzon, ed., *Globalization and Indigenous Culture* (Institute for Japanese Culture and Classics, 1997); and Roger Schlesinger, *In the Wake of Columbus: The Impact of the New World on Europe 1492-1650* (Harland Davidson, Inc., 1996).

10. Nearly all writings by Indigenous authors speaking to Indigenous matters, whether in the United States or the Republic of Mexico, contribute to the critical effort to define Indigeneity. On the United States, recent anthologies present a variety of views, the most recent being Anne Waters, ed., *American Indian Thought* (Blackwell, 1994). For three distinctly different statements on Indigenous definitions, see Ward Churchill, "I Am Indigenist," in Ward Churchill's *Struggle for the Land* (Common Courage, 1983); Hazel W. Hertzberg, *The Search for an American Indian Identity* (Syracuse University Press, 1971); and Pedro Carrasco, "Social Organization of Ancient Mexico," in *Handbook of Middle American Indians*, Vol. 10 (editors G. F. Ekholm and Ignacio Bernal, University of Texas, Austin: 1971). For a different tack, see Pauline Turner Strong, "Indian Blood: Reflections on the Reckoning and Refiguring of North American Identity," *Cultural Anthropology* Vol. 11 (November, 1996). For a different approach to Indigeneity than these titles, see Arturo Meza Gutiérrez, *Mosáico de Turquezas* (n.p., 1994).

11. The literature on perception of the Indigenous begins with the initial encounters with Europe; as to how Indigenous are affected and respond contemporarily, see Linda Tuhiwai Smith, *Decolonizing Methodologies* (Zed Books, 1999); Robert Allen Warrior, *Tribal Secrets: Recovering American Indian Intellectual Traditions* (University of Minnesota Press, 1994); Anne Waters, ed., *American Indian Thought* (Blackwell, 1994); and Andrea Smith, *Conquest, Sexual Violence and American Indian Genocide* (South End Press, 2005). For a scholarly examination of early contacts, see Louise M. Burkhart, *The Slippery Earth: Nahua-Christian Moral Dialogue in Sixteenth Century Mexico* (University of Arizona Press, 1989).

12. The literature on Indigenous as colonial subjects is large and growing. To begin, see J. M. Blaut, *The Colonizers Model of the World* (Guiliford Press, 1993). For Native's experiences under colonial rule, see James Lockhart, *The Nahuas After the Conquest: A Social and Cultural History of the Indians of Central Mexico* (Stanford University Press, 1992); Kevin Terraciano, *The Mixtecs of Colonial Oaxaca* (Stanford University Press, 2001); Charles Gibson, *Aztecs Under Spanish Rule* (Stanford University Press, 1964); Nancy

M. Farriss, *Maya Society Under Colonial Rule: The Collective Enterprise of Survival* (Princeton University Press, 1984); and Daniel K. Richter, *Facing East From Indian Country: A Native History of Early America* (Harvard University Press, 2001). For an overall survey, see John E. Kicza, *Resilient Cultures: America's Native Peoples Confront European Colonization 1500-1800* (Prentice Hall, 2003); and for a government's impact, see Francis Paul Prucha, *The Great Father: The United States Government and the American Indians* (University of Nebraska Press, 1986).

13. For the relation between epistemology and domination, see Linda Tuhiwai Smith, *Decolonizing Methodologies* (1999); Edward Said, *Orientalism* (Pantheon, 1978); Ward Churchill, "White Studies: The Intellectual Imperialism of Contemporary U.S. Education," *Integrateducation*, Vol. 19 (1982); and F. Apffel-Marglin and S. A. Marglin, eds., *Dominating Knowledge, Development Culture and Resistence* (Clarendon Press, 1990).

14. For direction on the complicated discourses on race, see M. Omi & H. Winant, *Racial Formation in the United States* (Routledge, 1994); David Theo Goldberg, *Racist Culture: Philosophy and the Politics of Meaning* (Blackwell: 1993); and Ashley Montagu, *Man's Most Dangerous Myth: The Fallacy of Race* [6th. ed.] (Alta Mira Press, 1997). For reviews of some of the literature by writers trying to sort out culture and race, see Reginald Horsman, "Well-Trodden Paths and Fresh Byways: Recent Writing on Native American History," *Reviews in American History*, Vol. 10 (December, 1982). For how Native Americans are set aside in discussions of race in the United States, see for example Steve Russell, "A Black and White Issue: The Invisibility of American Indians in Racial Policy Discourse," *Georgetown Public Policy Review*, Vol. 4 (1997). In Mexico, denial of race and racism has its own interpretations of denial, see G. Bonfil Batalla, *México Profundo* (Edition in English, University of Texas Press, 1996). For my discussion on race discourse among Mexicans historically in Mexico, see Juan G.-Quiñones, "A Triangular Paradigm of Hybridities and Racisms Among Mexicans," in Wm. Little, S. W. Williams, Irene Vásquez M., et al., *The Borders in All of Us: New Approaches to Global Diasporic Societies* (New World African Press, 2006).

15. For a study attempting a borderlands people's focus, see Walter D. Mignolo, *Local Histories/Global Designs* (Princeton University Press, 2000); and for a study focusing on the impact of images and representations on various social sectors among Mexicans, see Serge Gruzinski, *Images at War* (Duke University Press, 1990). These two highly touted studies are somewhat old wines in old bottles with new labels and are actually variants of Eurocentric post-colonial studies which continue to be Eurocentric. For what colonial borders actually inspired from another perspective, see Donna J. Guy and Thomas E. Sheridan, eds., *Contested Ground: Comparative Frontiers on the Northern and Southern Edges of the Spanish Empire* (University of Arizona Press, 1998). Now if the interests are on human life lived on borderlands as Indigenous, see James F. Brooks, *Captives and Cousins* (University of North Carolina Press, 2002); or Laura Velasco Ortiz, *Desde que tengo memoria* (CONACULTA, 2005).

16. For what is Indigenous as a historical question, see M. Annette Jaimes, "American Indian Studies: Toward an Indigenous Model," *American Indian Culture and Research Journal*, Vol. 11 (1987); R. Dunbar-Ortiz, "The Fourth World and Indigenism . . .," *Journal of Ethnic Studies*, Vol. 12 (Spring, 1984); Pedro Carrasco and Johanna Broda, eds., *Economía política e ideológica en el México prehispano* (Centro de Estudios Superiores del INAH, Editorial Nueva Imagen. México D.F.: 1978); and Jacques Soustelle, *The Four Suns* (1971). Also see Michael K. Green, ed., *Issues in Native American Cultural Identity* (P. Lang, 1995).

17. For references in the standard literature to science, see Luis Ortiz-Franco and María Magaña, "La ciencia de los antiguos Mexicanos," *Aztlan*, Vol. 4 (Spring, 1973). For discussion of science, see Alfred López Austin, *The Human Body and Ideology*, and also essays in Anne Waters, ed., *American Indian Thought* (1994); see also sections in Arturo Mesa Gutiérrez, *Mosáico de Turquezas* (1994). On views of time, see the traditional N. Scott Momaday, *The House Made of Dawn* (Harper & Row, 1968); the scholarly Laura Ibarra García, *La visión del mundo de los antiguos Mexicanos* (Universidad de Guadalajara, 1995); and the synthetic M. León-Portilla, *Native Mesoamerican Spirituality* (Paulist Press, 1980). Excellent is M.

León-Portilla, *Time and Reality in the Thought of the Maya* (Beacon Press, 1968). Some of the essays in Calvin Martin, ed., *The American Indian and the Problem of History* (Oxford University Press, 1987), take up the question of time along anecdotal lines.

18. For Indigenous views on history, see Miguel León-Portilla, *Aztec Thought and Culture* (University of Oklahoma Press, 1963); Dennis Tedlock, trans., *Finding the Center: Narrative Poetry of the Zuni Indians* (University of Nebraska Press, 1978); Gerald Vizenor, "Socioacupuncture: Mythic Reversals, and the Striptease in Four Scenes," in Calvin Martin, ed., *The American Indian and the Problem of History* (Oxford University Press, 1987); and for distant analogies, see Dipesh Chakrabarty, "Post Coloniality and the Artifice of History: Who Speaks for Indian Pasts?" [India], *Representations* Vol. 32 (Winter, 1992).

19. For some Indigenous space perspectives, see Alfredo López Austin, *Human Body and Ideology,* Vol. 1 (University of Utah Press, 1988); Laura Ibarra García, *Visión de los Antiguos Mexicanos*; and Jacques Soustelle, *Pensamiento cosmológico de los antiguos Mexicanos, representación del mundo y el espacio* (trans. María Elena Landa, Federación Estudiantil Poblana, 1959); and several of the essays in Calvin Martin, ed., *The American Indian and the Problem of History* (Oxford University Press, 1987).

20. On meta history tracts, see Richard E. W. Adams, *Prehistoric Mesoamerica* (1991); and Alfredo López Austin and Leonardo López Luján, *El Pasado Indígena* (1996).

21. On power relations and Indigenous governances, see James Lockhart, *The Nahuas After the Conquest* (1992); Kevin Terraciano, *The Mixtecs of Colonial Oaxaca* (2001); Thomas Biolsi, *Organizing the Lakota: The Political Economy of the New Deal on the Pine Ridge and Rosebud Reservations* (University of Arizona Press, 1992); Vine Deloria Jr. and Clifford Lytle, *The Nations Within: The Past and Future of Indian Sovereignty* (Pantheon, 1984); and Guillermo Bonfil Batalla, *México Profundo* (Edition in English, University of Texas Press, 1996).

22. On historical experiences of governance, see "Estas son las leyes que tenían los indios de la Nueva España," in Juan Bautista Pomar and Alonso de Zurita, *Relaciones de Texcoco y de la Nueva España* (Editorial Chávez Hayhoe, 1941); Guillermo Bonfil Batalla, *México Profundo* (1996); and Ignacio Romerovargas Iturbe, *Los Gobiernos Socialistas de Anáhuac* (Sociedad Cultural ITIT, 2000); also Roxanne Dunbar Ortiz, ed., *The Great Sioux Nation* (American Indian Treaty Council Information Center, 1977); and Dorothy V. Jones, *License for Empire: Colonialism By Treaty in Early America* (University of Chicago Press, 1982).

23. On Indigenous schooling experiences, see Henry Warner Bowden, *American Indians and Christian Missions: Studies in Cultural Conflict* (University of Chicago Press, 1981); also Hazel W. Hertzberg, *The Search for an American Indian Identity* (Syracuse University Press, 1971); Karen Gayton Swisher, "Why Indian People Should be the Ones to Write about Indian Education," in Devon A. Mihesuah, ed., *Natives and Academics* (University of Nebraska Press, 1998); and Philip G. Altback, "Education and Neocolonialism," *Teachers College Record*, Vol. 72 (May, 1971). There is the classic Robert Ricard, *The Spiritual Conquest of Mexico* (University of California Press, 1966). See also the insights and data of Pablo González Casanova, *La Democracia en México* (ERA, 1965), in particular the section in chapter 5, "La sociedad plural."

24. On Indigenous-Mestizo-African relations, see Luz María Martínez Montiel, ed., *Presencia Africana en México* (Dirección General de Culturas Populares, 1994); Jack Forbes, *Africans and Native Americans* (University of Illinois Press, 1993); Eric Wolf, *Sons of the Shaking Earth* (University of Chicago, 1959); and Guillermo Bonfil Batalla, *México Profundo* (1996). For a provocative discussion on ethnicity development as old and new, see Stuart Hall, "New Ethnicities," in David Morley and Kuan-Hsing Chen, eds., *Stuart Hall: Critical Dialogues in Cultural Studies* (Routledge, 1996).

25. On new and old theorizing, see Linda T. Smith, *Decolonizing Methodologies* (1999); and John Berger and Jean Mohr, *Another Way of Telling* (Pantheon, 1982). For a classic romantic approach, see Mircea Eliade, *Cosmos and History: The Myth of the Eternal Return* (Harper & Row, 1959); and for a social science structuralist approach, see James N. Hill, "Prehistoric Social Organization in the American Southwest: Theory and Method"; and Edward P. Dozier, "Making Inferences from the Present to the Past," both in W. A. Longacre, ed., *Reconstructing Prehistoric Pueblo Societies* (1970). For a review of theorizing from a culturalist perspective, see Barbara Christian, "The Race for Theory," *Cultural Critique* (Vol. 6, 1987).

26. For Indigenous views on cosmology in relation to religion, see Alfredo López Austin, *Hombre-dios: Religión y política en el mundo Nahuatl* (UNAM, 1973); Miguel León-Portilla, *Native Mesoamerican Spirituality* (Paulist Press, 1980); Vine Deloria Jr., *God is Red* (Grosset and Dunlap, 1973); Jacques Soustelle, *Pensamiento cosmológico de los antiguos Mexicanos* (1959); and Doug Boyd, *Mad Bear: Spirit, Healing, and the Sacred in the Life of a Native American Medicine Man* (Simon and Schuster, 1994). For views different from those presented here by me on cosmology, see Jamake Highwater, *The Primal Mind: Vision and Reality in Indian America* (Harper and Row, 1981); and David Carrasco, *Religions of Mesoamerica: Cosmovision and Ceremonial Centers* (Harper and Row, 1990).

27. Among the crowded literatures on religion and spirituality, see Ake Hultkrantz, ed., *Belief and Worship in Native North America* (Syracuse University Press, 1981); Alfredo López Austin, *Hombre-dios* (1973); Vine Deloria Jr., *God is Red* (1973); Walter Capps, ed., *Seeing With a Native Eye: Essays on Native American Religion* (Harper and Row, 1976); Miguel León-Portilla, *Native Mesoamerican Spirituality* (1980); Susan Hazen-Hammond, *Spider Woman's Web* (Perigre, 1999); Joel W. Martin, *The Land Looks After Us* (Oxford University Press, 2001); and Joseph Epes Brown, *Teaching Spirits* (Oxford University Press, 2001). For a critical view of Anglo American's reaction to Indigenous religion historically and contemporarily, see Philip Jenkins, *Dream Catchers: How Mainstream America Discovered Native Spirituality* (Oxford University Press, 2004).

28. On Indigenous views of human nature, see Miguel León-Portilla, *Aztec Thought and Culture* (University of Oklahoma Press,

1963); Alfredo López Austin, *The Human Body and Ideology*, Vol. 1 (1988); Mercedes de la Garza, *El hombre en el pensamiento Nahuatl y Maya* (UNAM, Instituto de Investigaciones Filosóficas; 1978); Cheryl Claassen and Rosemary A. Joyce, eds., *Women in Prehistory: North American and Mesoamerica* (University of Pennsylvania Press, Philadelphia: 1997); Paula Gunn Allen, *The Sacred Hoop: Recovering the Feminine in American Indian Traditions* (Beacon Press, 1992); and *Grandmothers of the Light* (Beacon Press, 1991). See also Will Roscoe, ed., *Living the Spirit: A Gay American Indian Anthology* (St. Martin's Press, 1988); and Arturo Meza Gutiérrez, *Mosáico de Turquezas* (1994).

29. On Indigenous views on society, see Miguel León-Portilla, *Toltecayotl, aspectos de la cultura Nahuatl* (Fondo de Cultura Económica, 1980); Pedro Carrasco, "La sociedad Mexicana antes de la conquista," *Historia General de México* (4 vols., El Colegio de México, 1976); Alfonso Ortiz, *The Tewa World* (University of Chicago, 1969); Susan Kellogg, *Weaving the Past* (Oxford University Press, 2005); and Patrisia González, *The Mud People* (Chusma House Publications, 2003). See also Will Roscoe, *Changing Ones: Third and Fourth Genders in Native North America* (St. Martin's Press, 2000); and Arturo Meza Gutiérrez, *Mosáico de Turquezas* (1994).

30. On culture, aesthetics and ideology, see the section "Esthetics" in Anne Waters, ed., *American Indian Thought* (1994); or Miguel León-Portilla, *Aztec Thought and Culture* (1963); or Clyde Warrior, "We Are Not Free," in Alvin Josephy, ed., *Red Power* (McGraw Hill, 1971); Alfredo López Austin, *The Human Body and Ideology*, Vol. 1 (1988); and Francisco de la Peña Martínez, *Los Hijos del Sexto Sol* (INAH, 2002). For contemporary expressions and views, see Marie Louise Krumrine and Susan Clare Scott, eds., *Art and the Native American* (Penn State University Press, 2001); and Trudy Griffin-Pierce, *Earth is My Mother, Sky is My Father* (University of New Mexico Press, 1995).

31. On the arts, see Miguel Covarrubias, *The Eagle, the Jaguar and the Serpent: Indian Art of the Americas* (1954); *Indian Art of Mexico and Central America* (Knopf, 1957); Frederick J. Dockstader, *Indian*

Art in North America: Arts and Crafts (New York Graphic Society, Greenwich, 1961); Esther Pasztory, *Pre-Columbian Art* (Cambridge University Press, 1998); Henry B. Nicholson and E. Quiñones Keber, *Art of Aztec Mexico* (National Gallery, 1983); Jesús Jáurequi and Carlo Bonfiglioli, coordinators, *Las Danzas de Conquista*, Vol. I, *Mexico Contemporáneo* (Fondo de Cultura Económica, 1996); Charlotte Heth, ed., *Native American Dance: Ceremonies and Social Traditions* (Smithsonian Institution, Washington, D.C.: 1992); Miguel León-Portilla and Earl Shorris, eds., *In the Language of Kings, An Anthology of Mesoamerican Literature* (Norton, New York: 2001); David Treuer, *Native American Fiction: A User's Manual* (Graywolf Press, 2006); Joy Harjo and Gloria Bird, eds., *Reinventing the Enemy's Language: Contemporary Native Women's Writings of North America* (Norton: 1997); W. Jackson Rushing III, ed., *Native American Art in the Twentieth Century* (Routledge, 1999); and Sherry L. Smith, *Reimagining Indians* (Oxford University Press, 2000).

32. On Indigenism and Human Rights, see several works by Roxanne Dunbar-Ortiz and Gaspar Rivera-Salgado.

33. On Indigenous views on ethics, see Miguel León-Portilla, *Aztec Thought and Culture* (1963); Walter H. Capps, ed., *Seeing with a Native Eye: Essays on Native American Religion* (Harper & Row, 1976); John Fire [Lame Deer] and Richard Erdoes, *Lame Deer, Seeker of Visions* (Simon and Schuster, 1972); and Joseph M. Marshall III, *The Lakota Way* (Penguin Compass, 2001).

34. On diagnosis of Indigenous internal relations, see Vine Deloria Jr., "American Indians and the Moral Community," *Church and Society*, Vol. 3 (September-October, 1988); Silvia J. Ramírez Romero, *La reconstrucción de la identidad política del Frente Indígena Oaxaqueño Binacional* (CNDPI, 2003); Paul C. Smith and Robert A. Warrior, *Like a Hurricane* (New Press Publishers, 1996); and Duane Champagne, *American Indian Societies* (Cultural Survival, 1989).

35. On Indigenous critiques, see Devon A. Mihesuah, ed., *Natives and Academics...*(University of Nebraska Press, 1998); Margot Liberty, ed., *American Indian Intellectuals: 1976 Proceedings of the*

American Ethnology Society West (St. Paul, 1978); Gerald Vizenor, *Narrative Chance: Postmodern Discourse on Native American Indian Literatures* (University of New Mexico Press, 1988); Gaspar Rivera-Salgado, "Equal in Dignity and Rights: The Struggle of Indigenous Peoples of the Americas," (Universiteit Utrecht, 2005); Alvin M. Josephy, Joane Nagel and Troy Johnson, eds., *Red Power* (University of Nebraska Press, 1999); and James Treat, *Around the Sacred Fire* (Polgrave MacMillan, 2003).

Bibliographical Note on the Literature Inspected and Interpretations Rejected

 **Learning**

Taking a long view of my interest in meanings of the Indigenous heritage, the trajectory stretches lengthy and curvy. I recall a moment quite clearly visiting with my colleague, Arturo Madrid, in Washington, D.C. where we viewed exhibitions on Matisse, South American folk art, and a small one on Pre-Columbian Panamanian gold art. This last exhibit was the most valuable. I realized the power of Indigenous art in juxtaposition to the other two. We avidly discussed the meaning of what we saw beyond the bare details of museum cards. We both recalled an older friend who became a best-selling author who discussed with us his field research on Yaqui ethnography when we gathered at the then upstairs lounge of the graduate reading room at the UCLA Powell Library. We agreed that Indigenous intellectual heritage, whether from the Peruvian and Mesoamerican highlands, was insufficiently known, as Carlos Mariategui pointed out many decades ago.

Many years later I was able to listen carefully to maestros Andrés Segura and Tata Cuaxtle, and years after that was deeply impressed by the work of the Seventh Generation Fund for Indian Development. Setting aside activist participations involving Native Americans and Indigenous representations, I did have several academic encounters related to the Indigenous from which I benefitted and thus appreciated, these involved faculty in the UCLA Anthropology Department: Professors Ralph L. Beals (Indigenous Community Studies), Johannes Wilbert (Native South American Folklore), and Henry J. Nicolson (Mesoamerican Peoples – Art and Religion). I also listened and read commentaries by Professor James A. Hill on Pueblo (Southwest) social organization and pertinent theories and methods. In my studies or readings with them I was a realist, now I am more critical. I have reflected upon many Indigenous exhibits and sites and have invariably been deeply impressed, whether in New Mexico or Oaxaca. I was able to visit many of these while a resident in Mexico City and also I learned much from my stay in Albuquerque, courtesy of the Center for Regional Studies, University of New Mexico, and Dr. Tobias Durán.

The extant literature on the Indigenous are multiple and diverse and the available film documentaries are important research assets. The overall literature which examines the Indigenous populations discretely is of course relatively large and is organizable along a variety of historiographical lines. That which examines Indigenous historical interaction internally is much less frequent. Literature which addresses Indigenous interactive processes transnationally, spoken by Indigenous individuals and groups, is available but scarce. For the purposes of these essays the interest is on literature pertinent to central and greater Mesoamerica. Many of the current scholarship extant findings may need to be extended and revised. Some of the demographic/regional/cultural assertions in some of the past scholarship are not tenable. The recurrent interpretations asserted for inter-ethnic relations, and the frequent stress on conflict must be supplemented and enriched by cultural and political expositions. Surely the literature is improving as a result of the salutary influence of maestros who teach via the spoken word and the writings of scholars empathetic to the Indigenous heritage.

Juan Gómez-Quiñones

Bibliography for Indigenous Quotient/Stalking Words

Acosta Figueroa, Alfredo. *Ancient Footprints of the Colorado River: La Cuna de Aztlán*. Aztec Printing Co., National City, CA: 2002.

Adams, Richard W. *Prehistoric Mesoamerica*. University of Oklahoma Press, Norman: 1998.

Akwesasne Notes. *A Basic Call to Consciousness: The Hau de no sau nee Address to the Western World*. Roosevelt Town, New York: 1978.

Allen, Paula Gunn. *Grandmothers of the Light*. Beacon Press, 1991.

Allen, Paula Gunn. *The Sacred Hoop: Recovering the Feminine in American Indian Traditions*. Beacon Press, 1992.

Altback, Philip G. "Education and Neocolonialism." In *Teachers College Record*, Vol. 72 (May, 1971).

Alva Ixtlilxochitl, Fernando de. *Obras Históricas*, edited by E. O'Gorman, UNAM, México D.F.: 1975-1977.

Alva, J. Jorge Klor de, et al. *The Life and Work of Bernardino de Sahagún*. State University of New York, IMS, 1988.

Alvarado Tezozomoc, Fernando de. *Crónica Mexicana* (1944 edition) and *Crónica Mexicayotl* (1949 edition). Also edition by Manuel Orozco y Berra, (precedida de *Códice Ramírez*), Editorial Porrúa, México D.F.: 1980.

Anderson, Arthur J. O., et al., eds. *Beyond the Codices: The Nahua View of Colonial Mexico*. University of California Press, Berkeley: 1976.

Apffel-Marglin, F., and S. A. Marglin, eds. *Dominating Knowledge, Development Culture, and Resistence*. Clarendon Press, 1990.

Appiah, Kwame Anthony. "The Post Colonial and the Post Modern." In K. A. Appiah, *In My Father's House: Africa in the Philosophy of Culture*. Methuen, 1992.

Arens, W. *The Man-Eating Myth: Anthropology and Anthropophagy*. Oxford University Press, 1979.

Armstrong, Gayle E. "Danza Azteca: Contemporary Manifestations of Danza de los Concheros in the United States." M.A. thesis in Dance, UCLA, 1985.

Assies, Willem, et al., eds. *The Challenge of Diversity: Indigenous*

Peoples and Reform of the State in Latin America. Thela Thesis, Amsterdam: 2000.

Axtell, James. "Columbian Encounters, 1992-1995." In *William and Mary Quarterly*, 3rd Ser., 52 (1995).

Bandelier, Fanny. *The Journey of Álvar Núñez Cabeza de Vaca*. Rio Grande Press, 1964.

Bataillon, Marcel. *Vasco de Quiroga et Bartolomé de las Casas*. Paris: 1965.

Baudot, Georges. *Utopía e historia en México: Los pimeros cronistas de la civilización Mexicana 1520-1569*. Espasa-Calpa, 1983.

Bauzon, Leslie E., ed. *Globalization and Indigenous Culture*. Institute for Japanese Culture and Classics, 1997.

Beals, Ralph. *Ethnology of the Western Mixe*. Cooper Square Publishers, New York: 1973.

Benítez, Fernando. *Los Indios de México*, 7 vols. ERA, México D.F.: 1991.

Benítez, Fernando. *Democracia Indígena*. ERA, México D.F.: 1972.

Berger, John, and Jean Mohr. *Another Way of Telling*. Pantheon, 1982.

Bhabha, Homi K. "Dissemination: Time, Narrative and the Margins of the Nodern Nation." In Homi K. Bhabha, ed. *Nation and Narration*. Routledge, 1990.

Biolsi, Thomas. *Organizing the Lakota: The Political Economy on the Pine Ridge and Rosebud Reservations*. University of Arizona Press, 1992.

Blanton, Richard E., et al. *Ancient Mesoamerica: A Comparison of Change in Three Regions*. Cambridge University Press, 1981.

Blaut, James. *The Colonizer's Model of the World: Geographical Diffusionism and Eurocentric History*. Guiliford Press, New York: 1993.

Bonfil Batalla, Guillermo. *Pensar Nuestra Cultura: Ensayos*. Alianza Editorial, México D.F.: 1991.

Bonfil Batalla, Guillermo. *México Profundo: Reclaiming a Civilization*. University of Texas Press, Austin: 1996.

Bonfil Batalla, Guillermo. "Sobre la ideología del mestizaje." In J. M. Valenzuela Arce, *Decadencia y auge de las identidades*, El Colegio de la Frontera Norte, Tijuana, B.C.: 1992.

Boone, Elizabeth Hill, and Tom Cummins, eds. *Native Traditions in the Post Conquest World.* Dumbarton Oaks Research Library, 1998.

Bordewich, Fergus M. *Killing the White Man's Indian: Reinventing Native Americans at the End of the Twentieth Century.* Doubleday, New York: 1996.

Bourne, Russell. *The Red King's Rebellion: Racial Politics in New England 1675-1678.* Oxford University Press, 1990.

Bowden, Henry Warner. *American Indians and Christian Missions: Studies in Cultural Conflict.* University of Chicago Press, 1981.

Boyd, Doug. *Mad Bear: Spirit, Healing, and the Sacred in the Life of a Native American Medicine Man.* Simon and Schuster, 1994.

Brooks, James F. *Captives & Cousins: Slavery, Kinship, and Community in the Southwest Borderlands.* University of North Carolina Press, Chapel Hill: 2002.

Brown, Dee. *Bury My Heart at Wounded Knee, An Indian History of the American West.* Vintage, New York: 1991.

Brown, Joseph Epes. *Teaching Spirits.* Oxford University Press, 2001.

Brown, Paula, and Donald F. Tuzin, eds. *The Ethnography of Cannibalism.* Society for Psychological Anthropology, Washington, D.C.: 1983.

Burkhart, Louise. *The Slippery Earth: Nahua-Christian Moral Dialogue in 16th Century Mexico.* University of Arizona Press, Tucson: 1989.

Bustamante, Carlos María de. *Cuadro histórico de la revolución de la América Mexicana,* 6 vols. (1823-1832).

Cabeza de Vaca, Álvaro Núñez. *Naufragios y Comentarios.* Taurus, Madrid: 1969.

Calloway, Colin G. *First Peoples: A Documentary Survey of American Indian History.* Bedford/St. Martins, Boston: 2004.

Cámara, Francisco López. "La conciencia criolla en Sor Juana y Sigüenza." In *Historia Mexicana,* Vol. 6 (1957).

Campa Mendoza, Víctor. *La problemática de las etnías en México.* Scienti Ediciones, no. pp., 1995.

Canny, Nicholas, and Kenneth Pagden, eds. *Colonial Identity in the Atlantic World 1500-1800.* Princeton University Press,

Princeton: 1987.

Capdequí, José Ma. Ots. *El Estado Español en las Indias*. Buenos Aires: 1952.

Capps, Walter H., ed. *Seeing With a Native Eye: Essays on Native American Religion*. Harper & Row, New York: 1976.

Carrasco, David. *Religions of Mesoamerica: Cosmovision and Ceremonial Centers*. Harper & Row, San Francisco: 1990.

Carrasco, Pedro. "La transformación de la cultura indígena durante la colonia." In *Historia Mexicana*, Vol. 25 (1975).

Carrasco, Pedro. "Social Organization of Ancient Mexico." In *Handbook of Middle American Indians*, Vol. 10. G. F. Ekholm and Ignacio Bernal, eds. University of Texas Press, Austin: 1971.

Carrasco, Pedro, and Johanna Broda, eds. *Economía política e ideológica en el México prehispanico*. INAH/ENI. México D.F.: 1978.

Casanova, Pablo. "La Sociedad Plural." In *La Democracia en México*. ERA, México D.F. : 1965.

Castile, George Pierre. *To Show Heart: Native American Self-Determination and Federal Indian Policy, 1960-1975*. University of Arizona Press, Tucson: 1998.

Chakrabarty, Dipesh. "Post Coloniality and the Artifice of History: Who Speaks for Indian Pasts?" In *Representations*, Vol. 32, India (Winter, 1992).

Champagne, Duane. *American Indian Societies: Some Strategies and Conditions of Political and Cultural Survival*. Cutural Survival, Inc., Boston: 1989.

Chipman, Donald E. "In Search of Cabeza de Vaca's Route Across Texas: An Historiographical Survey." In *Southwest Historical Quarterly*, Vol. 91 (1987).

Christian, Barbara. "The Race for Theory." In *Cultural Critique*, Vol. 6 (1987).

Churchill, Ward. "I Am Indigenist." In Ward Churchill's, *Struggle for the Land*. Common Courage, 1983.

Churchill, Ward. "White Studies: The Intellectual Imperialism of Contemporary U.S. Education." In *Integrateducation*, Vol. 19 (1982).

Claussen, Cheryl, and Rosemary A. Joyce, eds. *Women in Prehis-*

tory: *North American and Mesoamerica*. University of
Pennsylvania Press, Philadelphia: 1997.

Clavigero, Francisco Javier. *Historia Antigua de México*. R.P. Mariano Cuevas, ed. Porrúa, México D.F.: 1964.

Cline, H. F. *Handbook of North American Indians*. 1972-1975.

Closs, Michael P. *Native American Mathematics*. University of
Texas Press, Austin: 1996.

Cockcroft, James D. *Mexico's Hope: An Encounter with Politics and
History*. Monthly Review Press, New York: 1998.

Covarrubias, Miguel. *Indian Art of Mexico and Central America*.
Knopf, New York: 1957.

Covarrubias, Miguel. *The Eagle, the Jaguar and the Serpent: Indian
Art of the Americas*. Alfred A. Knopf, 1954.

Crow Dog, Leonard, with Richard Erdoes. *Crow Dog: Four Generations of Sioux Medicine Men*. Harper Perennial, New
York: 1995.

Cupryn, Teresa. "La expresión cósmica de la danza Azteca." In *Revista Mexicana de ciencias políticas y sociales*, Vol. 37, No.
147 (1992).

Deloria, Philip J. *Playing Indian*. Yale University Press, 1998.

Deloria Jr., Vine. "American Indians and the Moral Community." In
Church and Society, Vol. 3 (September-October, 1988).

Deloria Jr., Vine. *Custer Died for Your Sins*. University of Oklahoma
Press, Norman: 1988.

Deloria Jr., Vine. *God is Red*. Grosset and Dunlap, 1973.

Deloria Jr., Vine. *We Talk, You Listen: New Tribes, New Turf*. MacMillan, New York: 1970.

Deloria Jr., Vine, and Clifford Lytle. *The Nations Within: The Past
and Future of Indian Sovereignty*. Pantheon, 1984.

Denetdale, Jennifer Nez. "Representing Changing Woman: A
Review Essay on Navajo Women." In *American Indian
Culture and Research Journal*, Vol. 25 (2001).

Diamond, Jared. *Guns, Germs and Steel: The Fates of Human Societies*. W. W. Norton, New York: 1991.

Díaz de Jesús, Marcelino, et al., eds. *Alto Basas: Pueblos nahuas
en lucha por la autonomía, desarrollo y defensa de
nuestra cultura y territorio*. Consejo de Pueblos Nahuas del
Alto Basas, México D.F.: 1996.

Dickason, Olive Patricia. *Canada's First Nations*. Oxford University Press, 1997.

Dockstader, Frederick J. *Indian Art in North America: Arts and Crafts*. New York Graphic Society, Greenwich: 1961.

Dozier, Edward P. "Making Inferences from the Present to the Past." In W. A. Longacre, ed. *Reconstructing Prehistoric Pueblo Societies*. University of New Mexico Press, Albuquerque: 1970.

Dozier, Edward P. *The Pueblo Indians of North America*. Waveland Press, Prospect Heights, Illinois: 1970 & 1983.

Drinnon, Richard. *Facing West: The Metaphysics of Indian-Hating and Empire-Building*. University of Minnesota Press, Minneapolis: 1980.

Dunbar-Ortiz, Roxanne. *Indians of the Americas: Self-Determination and Human Rights*. Zed Books, London: 1984.

Dunbar-Ortiz, Roxanne. *Roots of Resistance: Land Tenure in New Mexico, 1680-1980*. CSRC/UCLA, Los Angeles: 1980.

Dunbar-Ortiz, Roxanne. *The Great Sioux Nation: Sitting in Judgement on America*. American Indian Treaty Council Information Center, Moon Books, New York/Berkeley: 1977.

Durán, Diego. *Book of the Gods and Rites and the Ancient Calendar*. University of Oklahoma Press, Norman: 1970.

Durham, Jimmie. *A Certain Lack of Coherence: Writings on Art and Cultural Politics*. Kala Press, London: 1993.

Edmunds, R. David, et al., eds. *The People: A History of Native America*. Houghton Mifflin, Boston: 2006.

Eguiara y Eguren, José de. *Prólogo de la Biblioteca Mexicana*. Agustín Millares Carlo, trans. México D.F.: 1944.

Eliade, Mircea. *Cosmos and History: The Myth of the Eternal Return*. Harper & Row, 1959.

Elias, Norbert. *The Civilizing Process*. Vol. 2, *State Formations and Civilization*. Pantheon Books, 1978.

Elliott, J. H. *Imperial Spain 1469-1716*. Mentor Book, New York: 1966.

El Oaxaqueño, Los Angeles, California, 2005-2006.

Estudios de Cultura Nahuatl. Vol. 1-18, 1959-1987, UNAM, México D.F.

Fanon, Frantz. *The Wretched of the Earth*. Grover, 1968.

Farrer, Claire Rafferty. *Living Life's Circle: Mescalero Apache Cosmovision*. University of New Mexico Press, Albuquerque: 1991.

Farriss, Nancy M. *Maya Society Under Colonial Rule: The Collective Enterprise of Survival*. Princeton University Press, 1984.

Fiedel, Stuart J. *Prehistory of the Americas*. Cambridge University Press, 1987.

Fine-Dare, Kathleen S. *Grave Injustice*. University of Nebraska Press, Lincoln: 2002.

Fire, John [Lame Deer], and Richard Erdoes. *Lame Deer, Seeker of Visions*. Simon and Schuster, New York: 1972.

Fisher, Marc. "Indian Museum's Appeal, Sadly, Only Skin Deep." In *Washington Post* (September 21, 2004).

Fixico, Donald L. "Ethics and Responsibilities in Writing American Indian History." In Devon A. Mihesuah, ed. *Natives and Academics: Research and Writing About American Indians*. University of Nebraska Press, Lincoln: 1998.

Florescano, Enrique, comp. *El Patrimonio Cultural de México*. Fondo de Cultura Económica. México D.F.: 1993.

Forbes, Jack D. *Africans and Native Americans*. University of Illinois Press, 1993.

Forbes, Jack D., ed. *The Indian in America's Past*. Prentice-Hall, Englewood Cliffs, NJ: 1964.

Fox, Jonathan, and Gaspar Rivera-Salgado, eds. *Indigenous Mexican Migrants in the United States*. Center for U.S.-Mexico Studies, UCSD, La Jolla: 2004.

Gamío, Manuel. *La Población del Valle de Teotihuacán*. 3 vols. Secretaría de Agricultura y Fomento, [Talleres Gráficos de la Nación] México D.F.: 1927.

Gamío, Manuel. *Forjando Patria: Pro-Nacionalismo* (1916). Editorial Porrúa, México D.F.: 1960.

Garibay Kintana, Ángel María. *Historia de la Literatura Náhuatl*, 2 vols. Editorial Porrúa, México D.F.: 1953-1954.

Garibay Kintana, Ángel María. *Poesía Náhuatl*. 3 vols. UNAM, México D.F.: 1963-1968.

Garza, Mercedes de la. *El hombre en el pensamiento religioso Maya y Nahuatl*. UNAM, México D.F.: 1978.

Gibson, Charles. *Aztecs Under Colonial Rule*. Stanford University Press, 1964.

Gibson, Charles. "Writings of Colonial Mexico." In *Hispanic American Historical Review*, Vol. 55 (1975).

Gish, Robert F. *Beyond Bounds: Cross Cultural Essays on Anglo, American Indian, & Chicano Literature*. University of New Mexico Press, Albuquerque: 1996 [See Part II].

Gómez-Quiñones, Juan. "A Triangular Paradigm of Hybridities and Racisms Among Mexicans." In Wm. Little, S. W. Williams, Irene Váquez M., et al. *The Borders in All of Us: New Approaches to Global Diasporic Societies*. New World African Press, 2006.

Gonzales, Patrisia. *The Mud People: Chronicles, Testimonios and Remembrances*. Chusma House Publications, San José: 2003.

González, María R. "El embrión nacionalista visto a través de la obra de Sor Juana..." In A. del Castillo, ed. *Between Borders*. Floricanto, Encino: 1990.

Gossen, Gary H. *Chamulas in the World of the Sun: Time and Space in a Maya Oral Tradition*. Harvard University Press, Cambridge: 1974.

Gossen, Gary H., ed. *Symbol and Meaning Beyond the Closed Community: Essays in Mesoamerican Ideas*. State University of New York, IMS, Albany: 1986.

Grajales, Gloria. *Nacionalismo incipiente en los historiadores coloniales*. UNAM, México D.F.: 1961.

Grande, Sandy Marie Anglas. "American Indian Geographies of Identity and Power: At the Crossroads of Indígena and Mestizaje." In *Harvard Educational Review*, Vol. 70 (Winter, 2000).

Green, Michael, ed. *Issues in Native American Cultural Identity*. P. Long, New York: 1995.

Griffin-Pierce, Trudy. *Earth is My Mother, Sky is My Father*. University of New Mexico Press, Albuquerque: 1995.

Gruzinski, Serge. *Images at War*. Duke University Press, 1990.

Guy, Donna J., and Thomas E. Sheridan, eds. *Contested Ground: Frontiers on the Northern and Southern Edges of the Spanish Empire*. University of Arizona Press, Tucson: 1998.

Guzmán, Eulalia, ed. *Relaciones de Hernán Cortés a Carlos V sobre la invasión de Anahuac*. Libros Anahuac, México D.F.: 1958.

Hall, Stuart. "New Ethnicities." In David Morley and Kuan-Hsing Chen, eds. *Stuart Hall: Critical Dialogues in Cultural Studies*. Routledge, 1996.

Hamill, Hugh M. *The Hidalgo Revolt: Prelude to Mexican Independence*. University of Florida Press, Gainesville: 1966.

Hamnett, Brian. "Mexico's Royalist Coalition: The Response to Revolution, 1808-1821." In *Journal of Latin American Studies*, Vol. 12 (1981).

Hanke, Lewis. *The Spanish Struggle for Justice in the Conquest of America*. Little, Brown & Company, Boston: 1965.

Hanke, Lewis. *Aristotle and the American Indians*. London: 1959.

Haring, C. H. *The Spanish Empire in America*. Harcourt, Brace & World, New York: 1963.

Harjo, Joy, and Gloria Bird, eds. *Reinventing the Enemy's Language: Contemporary Native Women's Writings of North America*. Norton, 1997.

Harris, Max. "The Return of Moctezuma: Oaxaca's Danza de la Pluma and New Mexico's Danza de los Matachines." In *The Drama Review*, Vol. 41 (Spring, 1997).

Hazen-Hammond, Susan. *Spider Woman's Web*. Perigree Trade, 1999.

Hedrick, Basil C., et al., eds. *The Mesoamerican Southwest: Readings in Archaeology, Ethnohistory and Ethnology*. Illinois University Press, Carbondale, IL: 1974.

Heredia, V. Beltrán de. *Los manuscritos del maestro Fray Francisco de Vitoria*. Madrid: 1928.

Hertzberg, Hazel W. *The Search for an American Indian Identity: Modern Pan Indian Movements*. Syracuse University Press, 1971.

Herzog, Jesús Silva. "Fray Servando Teresa de Mier." In *Cuadernos Americanos* (No. 154, 1967).

Heth, Charlotte, ed. *Native American Dance: Ceremonies and Social Traditions*. Smithsonian Institution, Washington D.C.: 1992.

Highwater, Jamake. *The Primal Mind: Vision and Reality in In-*

dian America. Harper & Row, New York: 1981.

Hill, James N. "Prehistoric Social Organization in the American Southwest: Theory and Method." In W. A. Longacre, ed. *Reconstructing Prehistoric Pueblo Societies*. University of New Mexico Press, Albuquerque: 1970.

Horowitz, David. *The First Frontier, The Indian Wars and America's Origins, 1607-1776*. Simon and Schuster, 1978.

Horsman, Reginald. *Expansion and American Indian Policy, 1783-1812*. University of Oklahoma Press, Norman: 1992.

Horsman, Reginald. "Well-Trodden Paths and Fresh Byways: Recent Writing on Native American History." In *Review in American History*, Vol. 10 (December, 1982).

Hoxie, Frederick E. *The Indians Versus the Textbooks: Is There Any Way Out?* Newberry Library, Chicago: 1984.

Hoxie, Frederick E. "The Problems of Indian History." In *Social Science Journal*, 25 (1988).

Huhndorf, Shari M. *Going Native*. Cornell University Press, 2001.

Hulme, Peter. "Columbus and the Cannibals." In *Colonial Encounters*. Methuen, London and New York: 1986.

Hultkrantz, Ake, ed. *Belief and Worship in Native North America*. Syracuse University Press, 1981.

Hurt, Douglas. *The Indian Frontier, 1763-1846*. University of New Mexico Press, Albuquerque: 2002.

Ibarra García, Laura. *La visión del mundo de los antiguos Mexicanos: Origen de sus conceptos de causualidad, tiempo y espacio*. Universidad de Guadalajara, Guadalajara, Jalisco: 1995.

Iwanska, Alicja. *The Truths of Others: An Essay on Nativistic Intellectuals in Mexico*. Schenkman Publishing, Cambridge, Mass.: 1977.

Jacobs, Sue-Ellen, et al., eds. *Two-Spirit People: Native American Gender Identity, Sexuality and Spirituality*. University of Illinois Press, Urbana: 1997.

Jaimes Guerrero, M. Annette. "Exemplars, Indigenism: Native North American Women for De/Colonization and Liberation." In Cathy J. Cohen, et al., *Women Transforming Politics*, New York University Press, New York: 1997.

Jaimes Guerrero, M. Annette. *The State of Native America*. South

End Press, Boston: 1992.

Jáuregui, Jesús, and Carlo Bonfiglioli, cords. *Las danzas de conquista: Vol. I. México Contemporáneo.* CONACULTA/ FCE, México D.F.: 1996.

Jenkins, Phillip. *Dream Catchers: How Mainstream America Discovered Native Spirituality.* Oxford University Press, 2004.

Jennings, Francis. *The Invasion of America: Indians, Colonialism, and the Cant of Conquest.* W. W. Norton, New York: 1976.

Jiménez Moreno, Wigberto. "Filosofía de la vida y transculturación religiosa: La religión Mexica y el Cristianismo." *Actas y Memorias XXXV, Congreso Internacional de Americanistas.* México D.F.: 1964.

Johnson, Troy, ed. *Contemporary Native American Political Issues.* AltaMira Press, Walnut Creek, CA: 1999.

Jones, Dorothy V. *License for Empire: Colonialism by Treaty in Early America.* University of Chicago Press, 1982.

Jones, Landon Y. *William Clark and the Shaping of the West.* Hill and Wang, New York: 2004.

Josephy, Alvin M. *Now That The Buffalo's Gone.* University of Oklahoma Press, Norman: 1985.

Josephy, Alvin M., Joane Nagel, and Troy Johnson, eds. *Red Power.* University of Nebraska Press, Lincoln: 1999.

Kehoe, Alice Beck. *America Before the European Invasions.* Longmen, New York: 2002.

Kellogg, Susan. "From Parallel and Equivalent to Separate but Unequal: Tenochca Mexica Women, 1500-1700." In Susan Schroeder, et al., eds. *Indian Women of Early Mexico.* University of Oklahoma Press, Norman: 1997.

Kellogg, Susan. *Weaving the Past: A History of Latin America's Indigenous Women.* Oxford University Press, Oxford: 2005.

Kicza, John E. *Resilient Cultures: America's Native Peoples Confront European Colonization.* Prentice Hall, 2003.

Kirchoff, Paul. "Mesoamérica: Sus límites geográficos, composición étnica y carácteres culturales." In *Acta Americana,* Vol. 1, 1943.

Klein, Kerwin. *Frontiers of Historical Imagination: Narrating the*

European Conquest of Native America. University of California Press, Berkeley: 1997.

Klor de Alva, Jorge. "The Aztec-Spanish Dialogues of 1524." In *Alcheringa*, Vol. 4 (1980).

Klor de Alva, Jorge. "Spiritual Conflict and Accommodation in New Spain: Toward a Typology of Aztec Responses to Christianity." In G. A. Collier, et al., *The Incan and Aztec States, 1400-1800.* Academics, New York: 1982.

Krumrine, Marie Louise, and Susan Clark Smith. *Art and the Native American.* Pennsylvania State University Press, University Park: 2001.

Krupat, Arnold. *Red Matters: Native American Studies.* University of Pennsylvania Press, Philadelphia: 2002.

Kuznesof, Elizabeth. "The History of the Family in Latin America: A Critique of Recent Work." In *Latin American Research Review*, Vol. 29 (1989).

Labastida, Jaime, and Jorge García Morineau. *El pensamiento mítico de los Coras.* Banrural, México D.F.: 1998.

Ladd, John. *The Structure of a Moral Code: A Philosophical Analysis of Ethical Discourse Applied to the Ethics of the Navajo Indians.* Harvard University Press, Cambridge, MA: 1957.

Lartigue, Francois, and André Quesnal, eds. *Las dinámicas de la población indígena: Cuestiones y debates actuales en México.* Centro de Investigaciones y Estudios Superiores en Antropología Social-Miguel Angel Porrúa, México D.F.: 2003.

Las Casas, Bartolomé de. *Apologética Historia Summaria.* 2 vols. UNAM, México D.F.: 1967.

Las Casas, Bartolomé de. *Historia de las Indias.* 3 vols. Fondo de Cultura Económica, México D.F.: 1951.

Leanord, Irving. *Baroque Times in Old Mexico.* University of Michigan Press, Ann Arbor: 1971.

León-Portilla, Miguel, and Earl Shorris, eds. *In the Language of Kings, An Anthology of Mesoamerican Literature, Pre-Columbian to the Present.* Norton, New York: 2001.

León-Portilla, Miguel. *Aztec Thought and Culture.* University of Oklahoma Press, Norman: 1963.

León-Portilla, Miguel. *Native Mesoamerican Spirituality.* Paulist

Press, New York: 1980.

León-Portilla, Miguel. *Pre-Columbian Literatures of Mexico*. University of Oklahoma Press, Norman: 1969.

León-Portilla, Miguel. *Time and Reality in the Thought of the Maya*. Beacon Press, Boston: 1973.

León-Portilla, Miguel. *Toltecayotl, Aspectos de la Cultura Náhuatl*. Fondo de Cultura Económica, México D.F.: 1980.

Lepore, Jill. *The Name of War: King Philip's War and the Origins of American Identity*. Knopf, New York: 1998.

Lestringant, F. "Calvinistes et cannibales." In *Bulletin de la Societe du protestantisme francais*, Nos. 1 & 2, 1980.

Liberty, Margot, ed. *American Indian Intellectuals: 1976 Proceedings of the American Ethnology Society West*. St. Paul, 1978.

Lockhart, James, et al., eds. *Annals of His Time: Don Domingo de San Antón Muñón Chimalpahin Quauhtlehuanitzin*. Stanford University Press, Stanford: 2006.

Lockhart, James. *The Nahuas After the Conquest*. Stanford University Press, Stanford: 1992.

Longacre, William A. *Reconstructing Prehistoric Pueblo Societies*. University of New Mexico Press, 1970.

López Austin, Alfredo. *Hombre-dios: Religión y política en el mundo nahuatl*. UNAM, México D.F.: 1998.

López Austin, Alfredo. *The Human Body and Ideology*. 2 vols. University of Utah Press, Salt Lake City: 1988.

López Austin, Alfredo. *The Myths of the Possum [Los Mitos del Tlacuache]*. University of New Mexico Press, 1990.

López Austin, Alfredo. "La sexualidad entre los antiguos Nahuas." In *Seminario de historia de mentalidades, familia y sexualidad en Nueva España*. SEP/80, México D.F.: 1982.

López Austin, Alfredo, and Leonardo López Luján. *El Pasado Indígena*. Fondo de Cultura Económica. México D.F.: 1996.

Losada, Ángel. *Juan Ginés de Sepúlveda a través de su "Epistolario" y nuevos documentos*. Madrid: 1959.

Lynch, Hohn. *Spain Under the Hapsburgs (1576-1700)*. 2 vols. Oxford University Press, New York: 1964, 1969.

Mares, Ernesto A. "Continuidad de la tradición filosófica nahuatl en las danzas de los Concheros." In *El Cuaderno*, Vol. 3 (1973).

Márez, Curtis. "Signifying Spain, Becoming Comanche, Making Mexicans." In *American Quarterly*, Vol. 53 (June, 2001).

Marshall, Joseph M. *The Lakota Way*. Penguin Compass, New York: 2001.

Marriott, Alice, and Carol K. Rachlin. *American Indian Mythology*. Crowell, New York: 1968.

Martin, Calvin, ed. *The American Indian and the Problem of History*. Oxford University Press, 1987.

Martin, Joel W. *The Lord Looks After Us*. Oxford University Press, 2001.

Martínez Parédez, Domingo. *El Popol Vuh tiéne razon, teoría sobre la cosmogonía preamericana*. Editorial Orión, México D.F.: 1976.

McNeley, James Kale. *Holy Wind in Navajo Philosophy*. University of Arizona Press, Tucson: 1981.

Mallon, Florencia. "The Promise and Dilemma of Subaltern Studies: Perspectives from Latin American History." In *American Historical Review*, Vol. 99 (1994).

Marshal, C. E. "The Birth of the Mestizo in New Spain." In *Hispanic American Historical Review*, Vol. 43 (1963).

Mathien, Frances Joan, and R. H. McGuire, eds. *Ripples in the Chichimec Sea: New Considerations in Southwestern-Mesoamerican Interactions*. Southern Illinois University Press, 1986.

Matthiessen, Peter. *In the Spirit of Crazy Horse: The Story of Leonard Peltier*. Viking, New York: 1991.

McMurtry, Larry. *In a Narrow Grave, Essays on Texas*. Simon and Schuster, New York: 1968.

McMurtry, Larry. *Sacagawea's Nickname, Essays on the American West*. New York Review of Books, New York: 2004.

Memoria del simposium nacional sobre el Primer Congreso Anauak (1964). SM de Gy E., México D.F.: 1964.

Menchaca, Martha. *Recovering History, Constructing Race: The Indian, Black and White Roots of Mexican Americans*. University of Texas Press, Austin: 2001.

Merrell, James H. "Some Thoughts on Colonial Historians and American Indians." In *William and Mary Quarterly*, 3rd Ser., 46 (1989).

Methvin, John Jasper. *Andele, or, The Mexican-Kiowa Captive.* University of New Mexico Press, Albuquerque: 1996.

Meza Gutiérrez, Arturo. *La incógnita del nombre de México.* Kalpulli Toltch Kayotl, np., nd.

Meza Gutiérrez, Arturo. *Mosáico de Turquesas.* Ediciones Artesanales Mallinalli, México: 1994.

Meza Gutiérrez, Arturo. *Tezkatlipoka: Nuestro Ser Interno.* Universidad Michoacana, Morelia: 1997.

Mier, Fray Servando Teresa de. *Escritos Inéditos.* México D.F.: 1944.

Mier, Fray Servando Teresa de. *Historia de la revolución de Nueva España.* Imprenta de la Cámara de Diputados, México D.F.: 1922.

Mignolo, Walter D. *Local Histories/Global Designs: Coloniality, Subaltern Knowledges, and Border Thinking.* Princeton University Press, Princeton: 2000.

Mignolo, Walter D. *The Darker Side of the Renaissance.* University of Minnesota Press, Minneapolis: 1995.

Mihesuah, Devon Abbott. *Indigenous American Women.* University of Nebraska Press, Lincoln: 2003.

Mihesuah, Devon Abbott. *Natives and Academics: Researching and Writing about American Indians.* University of Nebraska Press, Lincoln: 1998.

Miller, Virginia E., ed. *The Role of Gender in Pre-Columbian Art and Architecture.* University Press of America, Lanham, MD: 1988.

Mirafuentes Galván, José Luís. *Movimientos de resistencia y rebeliones indígenas en el norte de México 1680-1821.* 2 vols. UNAM, México D.F.: 1989 & 1993.

Moises, Rosalio, et al. *A Yaqui Life: The Personal Chronicle of a Yaqui Indian.* University of Nebraska Press, Lincoln: 1971.

Momaday, N. Scott. *House Made of Dawn.* Harper and Row, New York: 1968.

Momaday, N. Scott. *The Man Made of Words.* St. Martin's Press, 1991.

Montagu, Ashley. *Man's Most Dangerous Myth: The Fallacy of Race.* Alta Mira Press, 1997.

Montiel, Luz María Martínez, ed. *Presencia Africana en México.* Dirección General de Culturas Populares, 1994.

Morner, Magnus. *Race Mixture in the History of Latin America.* Little, Brown & Company, Boston: 1967.

Nagel, Joane. *American Indian Ethnic Renewal: Red Power and the Resurgence of Identity and Culture.* Oxford University Press, New York: 1996.

Namala, Doris. "Chimalpahin in His Time: An Analysis of a Nahua Annalist of Seventeenth Century Mexico Concerning His Own Lifetime." Ph.D. dissertation, UCLA, 2002.

Navajo Times. "Delegation Confronts Lewis and Clark Re-enactors." (September 23, 2002).

Neihardt, John G. *Black Elk Speaks: Being the Life Story of a Holy Man of the Oglala Sioux.* Simon and Schuster, New York: 1972.

Nicholson, Henry B., and E. Quiñones Keber. *Art of Aztec Mexico.* National Gallery, 1983.

Nieva, María del Carmen. *Mexikayotl* (Esencia del Mexicano; Filosofía Nahuatl). Editorial Orión, México, D.F.: 1969.

Nieva López, María del Carmen. *Izkalotl Texto: Nahuatl-Español-Inglés.* np. Mexico-Tenochtitlan: 1972.

Noonan, John T., and Edward McGlynn Gaffney. *Religious Free dom.* Foundation Press, New York: 2001.

O, Jaime E. Rodríguez, ed. *The Independence of Mexico and Creation of the New Nation.* UCLA-LAC, Los Angeles: 1989.

Obregón, Luís González. *Rebeliones indígenas y precursores de la independencia Mexicana en los siglos XVI, XVII y XVIII.* Ediciones Fuente Cultural, México D.F.: 1952.

O'Gorman, Edmundo. *La Invención de América.* Fondo de Cultura Económica, México D.F.: 1958.

Oliver, Guilhem. "Los animales en el mundo prehispánico." *Arqueología Mexicana.* Vol. 6, No. 35 (enero-febrero, 1999).

Orozco y Berra, Manuel. *Noticia histórica de la conjuración del Marquez del Valle: Años 1565-1568.* México D.F.: 1853.

Ortiz, Alfonso. *The Tewa World: Space, Time and Becoming in a Pueblo Society.* University of Chicago Press, Chicago: 1969.

Ortiz, Simon J., and Rudolfo Anaya. *A Ceremony of Brotherhood, 1680-1980.* Academia, Albuquerque: 1981.

Ortiz, Simon J., and Elena Poniatowska. *Questions and Swords: Folktales of the Zapatista Revolution.* Cinco Puntos Press,

El Paso: 2001.

Ortiz-Franco, Luis, and María Magaña. "Ciencia de los Antiguos Mexicanos." In *Aztlan*, Vol. 4 (Spring, 1973).

Otis, D. S., ed. *The Dawes Act and the Allotment of Indian Lands*. University of Oklahoma Press, Norman: 1973.

Pagden, Anthony. *The Fall of Natural Man: The American Indian and the Origins of Comparative Ethnology*. Cambridge University Press, 1982.

Pagden, Anthony. *An Eighteenth Century Historian of Mexico: Francisco Javier Clavigero* and *Storia antica del Messico*. Leiden: 1983.

Parry, Benita. "The Scramble for Post Colonialism." In Chris Tiffin and Alan Lawson, eds. *De-Scribing Empire: Post-Colonialism and Textuality*. Routledge, 1994.

Pasztory, Esther. *Aztec Art*. Harry N. Abrams, New York: 1983.

Pasztory, Esther. *Pre-Columbian Art*. Cambridge University Press, Cambridge: 1998.

Pasztory, Esther. *Teotihuacan: An Experiment in Living*. University of Oklahoma Press, Norman: 1997.

Paz, Octavio. *Sor Juana Inés de la Cruz, las trampas de la fé*. Fondo de Cultura Económica, México D.F.: 1983.

Peña Martínez, Francisco de la. *Los Hijos del Sexto Sol*. INAH, México D.F.: 2002.

Phelan, John L. *The Millennial Kingdom of the Franciscans in the New World*. University of California Press, Berkeley: 1956.

Pizzigoni, Caterina. "Between Resistance and Assimilation: Rural Nahua Women in the Valley of Toluca in the Early Eighteenth Century." Ph.D. dissertation, King's College, University of London, 2002.

Pomar, Juan Bautista, and Alonso de Zurita. *Relaciones de Texcoco...* Editorial Chávez Hayhoe, 1941.

Poole, Stafford, trans. *In Defense of the Indians*. Northern Illinois University Press, De Kalb, IL: 1974.

Popol Vuh. [Ralph Nelson, trans.] Houghton, Boston: 1974.

Poveda, Pablo. "Danza de Concheros en Austin, Texas: Entrevista con Andrés Segura Granados." In *Latin American Music Review - Revista de Música Latinoamericana*, Vol. 2, No. 2 (1981).

Priest, Loring Benson. *Uncle Sam's Stepchildren: The Reformation of United States Indian Policy 1865-1887.* University of Nebraska Press, Lincoln: 1969.

Prucha, Francis Paul. *Documents of United States Indian Policy.* University of Nebraska Press, Lincoln: 1990.

Prucha, Francis Paul. *The Great Father: The United States Government and the American Indians.* University of Nebraska Press, Lincoln: 1986.

Quiñones Keber, Eloise, ed. *Representing Aztec Ritual.* University of Colorado Press, Boulder: 2002.

Quiroga, Vasco de. *Documentos.* Polis, México D.F.: 1939.

Radding, Cynthia. *Wandering Peoples: Colonialism, Ethnic Spaces, and Ecological Frontiers.* Duke University Press, 1997.

Ramírez Oropeza, Martha. "Huehuepohualli: Counting the Ancestor's Heartbeat." In D. Adams and A. Goldbard, eds. *Community, Culture, and Globalization.* The Rockefeller Foundation, New York: 2002.

Ramírez Romero, Silvia Jaquelina. *La reconstrucción de la identidad política del Frente Indígena Oaxaqueño Binacional.* Com. Nac. p.e. des. de los Pueblos Indígenas, México D.F.: 2003.

Ricard, Robert. *The Spiritual Conquest of Mexico.* University of California, Berkeley: 1966. Originally published in French, 1933.

Richter, Daniel K. *Facing East From Indian Country: A Native History of Early America.* Harvard University Press, 2001.

Richter, Daniel K. "Whose Indian History?" ibid., 50 (1993).

Ríos, Juan. "Indigenismo in the Urban Environment: A Discussion with Paztel Mireles, Aztec Dance Elder, Los Angeles, 1994." In *Raíces*, Vol. 1 (1995).

Rivera-Salgado, Gaspar. "Equal in Dignity and Rights: The Struggle of Indigenous Peoples of the Americas in an Age of Migration." Universiteit Utrecht, Netherlands: April 2005.

Rodríguez, Roberto, and Patrisia Gonzales. "Amoxtli San Ce Tojuan." *Chicano Records and Films*, San Fernando, CA: 2005.

Rogin, Michael Paul. *Fathers and Children, Andrew Jackson and the Subjugation of the American Indian.* Alfred A. Knopf, 1975.

Romerovargas Iturbe, Ignacio. *El Calpulli de Anahuac*. np., México D.F.: 1959.

Romerovargas Iturbe, Ignacio. *Los Gobiernos Socialistas del Anahuac*. Sociedad Cultural In Tlilli Tlapalli. México D.F.: 2000.

Romerovargas Iturbe, Ignacio. *La organización política de los pueblos de Anahuac*. np., México D.F.: 1957.

Roscoe, Will. *Changing Ones: Third and Fourth Genders in Native North America*. St. Martin's Press, New York: 1998.

Roscoe, Will, ed. *Living the Spirit: A Gay American Indian Anthology*. St. Martin's Press, New York: 1988.

Rushing, W. Jackson, ed. *Native American Art in the Twentieth Century*. Routledge, New York: 1999.

Russell, Steve. "A Black and White Issue: The Invisibility of American Indians in Racial Policy Discourse." In *Georgetown Public Policy Review*, Vol. 4 (1997).

Sacks, Karen. "Engels Revisited: Women, the Organization of Production and Private Property." In Michelle Zimbalist Rosaldo, et al. *Women, Culture and Society*. Stanford University Press, Stanford: 1974.

Sahagún, Fray Bernardino de. *General History of the Things of New Spain*. 12 vols. University of Utah Press, Salt Lake City: 1950-1969 [in particular the summary comments on *The Florentine Codex* as found in Miguel León-Portilla, *Native Mesoamerican Spirituality*, pp. 220-225].

Salisbury, Neal. *Manitou and Providence: Indian, Europeans, and the Making of New England, 1500-1643*. Oxford University Press, 1982.

Salisbury, Neal. "The Indian's Old World: Native Americans and the Coming of Europeans." In *The William and Mary Quarterly*, Vol. 53 (1996).

Salomón, Carlos. "Recent Impact of Transnational Indigenous Organizations in Mexico and the United States." In Irene Vásquez and D. O'Connor-Gómez, eds. *Proceedings of the Pacific Coast Council on Latin American Studies 2002-2003* PCCLAS (2005).

Savala, Refugio. *Autobiography of a Yaqui Poet*. University of Arizona Press, Tucson: 1980.

Schlesinger, Roger. *In the Wake of Columbus: The Impact of the New World on Europe 1492-1650*. Harland Davidson, Inc., 1996.

Schroeder, Susan. *Chimalpahin and the Kingdoms of Cholco*. University of Arizona, Tucson: 1991.

Schroeder, Susan, et al. *Indian Women of Early Mexico*. University of Oklahoma Press, Norman: 1997.

Séjourné, Laurette. *Burning Water: Thought and Religion in Ancient Mexico*. Thomas and Hudson, London: 1957.

Sepúlveda, Juan Ginés de. *Democrates, segundo, o de las justas causas de la guerra contra los Indios*. Instituto de Vitoria, Madrid: 1951.

Shoemaker, Nancy. *American Indian Population Recovery in the Twentieth Century*. University of New Mexico Press, 1999.

Sigüenza y Góngora, Carlos de. "Teatro de virtudes que constituyen a un príncipe." In *Obras*, Francisco Pérez Salazar, ed. México D.F.: 1928.

Silko, Leslie Marmon. *Ceremony*. The Viking Press, New York: 1977.

Smith, Andrea. *Conquest: Sexual Violence and American Indian Genocide*. South End Press, Cambridge: 2005.

Smith, Linda Tuhiwai. *Decolonizing Methodologies: Research and Indigenous Peoples*. Zed Books, London & New York: 1991.

Smith, Paul C., and Richard A. Warrior. *Like a Hurricane: The Indian Movement From Alcatraz to Wounded Knee*. New Press Publishers, New York: 1996.

Smith, Sherry L. *Reimagining Indians: Native Americans Through Anglo Eyes, 1880-1990*. Oxford University Press, 2000.

Sokolow, Jayme. *The Great Encounter: Native Peoples and European Settlers in the Americas, 1492-1800*. M. E. Sharp Publishers, Armonk, N.Y.: 2003.

Soustelle, Jacques. "Apuntes sobre la psicología y el sistema de valores en México antes de la conquista." In *Estudios Antropológicos . . . en honor del Dr. Manuel Gamío*. UNAM, México D.F.: 1950.

Soustelle, Jacques. *The Daily Life of the Aztecs*. Macmillan, New York: 1962.

Soustelle, Jacques. *The Four Suns: Recollections and Reflections of an Ethnologist in Mexico.* Grossman Publishers, New York: 1971.

Soustelle, Jacques. *Pensamiento cosmológico de los antiguos Mexicanos, representación del mundo y del espacio* (trans. M. E. Land A.). Federación Estudiante Poblana, Puebla, México: 1959.

Spivak, Gayatri Chakravorty. "Can the Subaltern Speak?" In Cary Nelson and Lawrence Grossbert, eds. *Marxism and the Interpretation of Culture.* MacMillan, 1988; or *In Other Worlds: Essays in Cultural Politics.* Routledge, 1988.

Spore, Ronald. "Mixteca Cacicas: Status, Wealth and Political Accommodation of Native Elite Women in Early Colonial Oaxaca." In Susan Schroeder, et al. *Indian Women of Early Mexico.* University of Oklahoma Press, Norman: 1999.

Stampa, Manuel Carrera. "Historiadores indígenas y mestizos novohispanos, siglos XVI-XVII." In *Revista Española*, Vol. 6 (1971).

Stedman, Raymond W. *Shadows of the Indian: Stereotypes in American Culture.* University of Oklahoma Press, Norman: 1982.

Suárez, Francisco. *Conselhos e Pareceres.* 2 vols. Coimbra, 1953.

Swisher, Karen Gayton. "Why Indian People Should be the Ones to Write about Indian Education." In Devon A. Mihesuah, ed. *Natives and Academics.* University of Nebraska Press, Lincoln: 1998.

Taylor, Graham D. *The New Deal and American Indian Tribalism: The Administration of the Indian Reorganization Act, 1934-45.* University of Nebraska Press, Lincoln: 1980.

Tedlock, Dennis, tr. *Finding the Center: Narrative Poetry of the Zuni Indian.* University of Nebraska Press, Lincoln: 1978.

Tedlock, Dennis, tr. *Popol Vuh: The Mayan Book of the Dawn of Life.* Simon and Schuster, New York: 1985.

Tedlock, Dennis, and Barbara Tedlock, eds. *Teachings from the American Earth: Indian Religion and Philosophy.* Liveright, New York: 1975.

Terraciano, Kevin. *The Mixtecs of Colonial Oaxaca.* Stanford University Press, Stanford: 2001.

Thomas, David Hurst, et al. *The Native Americans: An Illustrated History*. Turner Publishing, Atlanta: 1993.

Todorov, Tzvetan. *The Conquest of America: The Question of the Other*. Harper Perennial, New York: 1984.

Treat, James. *Around the Sacred Fire*. Polgrave MacMillan, 2003.

Treuer, David. *Native American Fiction: A User's Manual*. Graywolf Press, 2006.

Trueba, Alfonso, ed. *Doña Eulalia, el mestizo y otros temas*. Editorial Jus, México D.F.: 1959.

Tsosie, Rebecca. "Changing Women: The Cross-Currents of American Indian Feminine Identity." In Vicki L. Ruiz, et al. *Unequal Sisters*. Routledge, New York: 2000.

Tsosie, Rebecca. "Surviving the War by Singing the Blues: The Contemporary Ethos of American Indian Political Poetry." In *American Indian Culture and Research Journal*, Vol. 10 (1986).

Turner, Frederick Jackson. *The Significance of the Frontier in American History*. Harold P. Simonson, ed. Frederick Unger, New York: 1963.

Turner Strong, Pauline, and Barrik Van Winkle. "'Indian Blood': Reflections on the Reckoning and Refiguring of Native North American Identity." In *Cultural Anthropology*, Vol. 11 (Special issue on Resisting Identities, November, 1996).

Utley, Robert. *The Indian Frontier of the American West, 1846-1890*. University of New Mexico Press, Albuquerque: 1984.

Utter, Jack. *American Indians: Answers to Today's Questions*. University of Oklahoma Press, Norman: 2001.

Valdés, Luz María. *Los indios en los censos de población*. UNAM.

Vitoria, Francisco de. *Reflecciones sobre los Indios*. Espasa Calpe, Buenos Aires: 1946.

Vitoria, Francisco de. *Obras de Francisco de Vitoria*. Madrid: 1960.

Vizenor, Gerald. *Narrative Chance: Postmodern Discourse on Native American Indian Literatures*. University of New Mexico Press, 1988.

Vizenor, Gerald. "Socioacupuncture: Mythic Reversals, and the Striptease in Four Scenes." In Calvin Martin, ed. *The American Indian and the Problem of History*. Oxford University Press, 1987.

Wallace, Anthony F. C. *Jefferson and the Indians: The Tragic Fate of the First Americans*. Harvard University Press, Cambridge: 1999.

Wallace, Anthony F. C. *The Death and Rebirth of the Seneca*. Vintage, New York: 1972.

Warrior, Robert Allen. *Tribal Secrets: Recovering American Indian Intellectual Traditions*. University of Minnesota Press, Minneapolis: 1994.

Waters, Anne, ed. *American Indian Thought: Philosophical Essays*. Blackwell, Oxford: 1994.

Waters, Frank, with Oswald White Bear Fredericks. *Book of the Hopi: The First Revelation of the Hopi's Historical and Religious View of Life*. Ballantine Books, New York: 1963.

Weber, David. *The Spanish Frontier in North America*. Yale University Press, 1992.

Weston, Rubin F. *Racism in U.S. Imperialism*. University of South Carolina Press, 1972.

White, Richard. *The Roots of Dependency: Subsistence, Environment and Social Change Among the Choctows, Pawnees and Navajo*. University of Nebraska Press, Lincoln: 1983.

Wilkins, David. *American Indian Politics and the American Political System*. Rowland and Littlefield, Lanham, MD: 2002.

Witherspoon, Gary. *Language and Art in the Navajo Universe*. University of Michigan Press, Ann Arbor: 1977.

Wolf, Eric. *Sons of the Shaking Earth*. University of Chicago Press, Chicago: 1959.

Zavala, Silvio. *La filosofía política en la conquista de México*. Editorial Cultura, México D.F.: 1947.

Zavala, Silvio. *La utopía de Tomás Moro en la Nueva España*. México D.F.: 1957.

Zea, Leopoldo. *El Pensamiento Latinoamericano*, 2 vols. Editorial Pormoca, México D.F.: 1965.

Zimbalist Rosaldo, Michelle. "Women, Culture, and Society: A Theoretical Overview." In *Women, Culture and Society*. Stanford University Press, Stanford: 1974.

About the Author

Juan Gómez-Quiñones is an award-winning educator, author, community activist, editor, poet, and for over forty years, one of the foremost Chicano historians and scholars in the U.S. He received his Ph.D. from the University of California Los Angeles where he is currently a Professor of History, and where he has taught since 1974. He specializes in the fields of political, labor, intellectual, and cultural history. Among his over thirty published writings, that include articles and monographs, are the books: *Mexican American Labor: 1790-1990*; *The Roots of Chicano Politics: 1600-1940*; *Chicano Politics: 1940-1990*; and *5th and Grande Vista* (poetry).